GARDENING
The Complete Beginner's Guide

Gardeners' World

GARDENING
The Complete Beginner's Guide

How to Garden in Ten Easy Steps

BOOKS

CHAPTER ONE

Take the time to plan

Take the time to plan

Left: Colourful seating makes an impact in a small garden

It's a daunting prospect: there it sits, this patch of land that's optimistically called 'a garden', and it will be either an intimidating blank canvas or a mishmash of inherited features that don't suit you one bit. The temptation is to tackle just one corner, to blast away and blitz it, then retire to the house and collapse in a heap, not convinced you've achieved anything.

What you need is a master plan, but how do you make one when you're not at all sure what such a thing is? The answer is to take things one step at a time. You probably have an idea of what you want, but before you go any further, take a look at what you've got.

By assessing the situation accurately you can hopefully avoid wasted time, effort and money. Then, wherever your patch of ground is, and whatever it looks like, it will be possible to turn it into a garden that's worthy of the name, provided you tackle it in the right way.

Core skills:
– Soil testing
– Improving soil
– Working out how the aspect of your garden will affect it

5 steps to success

Right: Curved paths add interest to a rectangular garden

(1) **First check the boundaries** of the plot and see if the fence panels are sound. Having to replace them after you've made your garden would risk damaging what you've already created. Those 6ft x 6ft interwoven panels are notorious for blowing over in strong winds, so check the posts aren't rotten at the base. Concrete posts are much more durable, and new panels can be slid into the slots to replace old, rotting ones in the future.

(2) **Get out there with a tape measure** and jot down the size and shape of your plot. You don't have to be a professional draughtsman to sketch out a plan, and looking at a sketch of the shape and working out what might go where will help to clarify things in your head. Mark the site of any drain covers and the path of the drains that link them, to avoid expensive damage.

(3) **Decide what to keep** and what to get rid of – if the garden already contains some things that you like, indicate their position on the plan so you can work around them. They might become a focal point for a path or a view. Similarly, decide which features or overgrown shrubs can be dispensed with. Sometimes it's hard to bite the bullet and get rid of an established plant. If it adds to the atmosphere of the garden and looks reasonably healthy, you might want to keep it. If it's ugly or overgrown, or you simply don't like the look of it, then get rid of it. If it's a tree, check whether it's subject to a Tree Preservation Order, in which case you'll have to keep it.

(4) **Tackle your garden at a pace that suits you.** If it's already established when you move in, allow time to see what comes up in spring and summer before going in with an earth mover and making drastic alterations. You may be pleasantly surprised at what you've inherited. Garden-making is a continuous journey, and it can and should be an enjoyable one – anything that's planted in the wrong place can always be moved. Remember that, and your stress levels will be greatly reduced.

(5) **Design your garden so it suits your lifestyle**. If your time is limited, restrict the number of borders, or fill them with plants that need little maintenance. The main features that will need regular attention are a fruit and veg plot and a greenhouse. Containers will require regular watering in spring and summer, although you could set up a drip irrigation system on an automatic timer.

What tools do you need?

Resist the temptation to buy umpteen gadgets. You really won't use them once the novelty has worn off. Your tool shed needs to contain only the essentials, unless you see yourself as a James Bond kind of gardener with all manner of complex implements at your disposal. Here are some of the most useful tools.

 Spade and fork – but if you're not built like a wrestler then choose a border spade and border fork, which are smaller (or preferably all four)

 Dutch hoe (long-handled hoe ideal for getting rid of annual weeds)

 Onion hoe (short-handled hoe for weeding between crops)

 Trowel and hand fork

 Dibber

 Garden line

 Sharp knife

 Sharp secateurs

 Hand shears

 Watering can

You may need:

 Wheelbarrow (for large gardens)

 Mower (battery powered if you want to be environmentally friendly – and quiet)

 Rake

 Kneeler

 Gardening gloves

 Pruning saw

 Loppers (good for pruning thicker stems)

 Half moon edging tool (to neaten up the sides of your lawn)

You can add to this list, but these will be the implements most frequently taken down off their hooks. Try to keep them clean, they're more pleasurable to use that way. Old tools are wonderfully tactile – they've been run in by a previous generation – but new ones are not to be dismissed. Comfort, balance and durability are the most important assets, so spend well on quality craftsmanship.

How to assess your garden

UNDERSTAND YOUR ASPECT

The 'aspect' is the direction your garden faces – north, south, east or west. This affects which areas get plenty of sun and which ones are thrown into shadow for all or part of the day. The simplest way to work out your aspect is to stand by the outside wall at the back of your house with a compass and see which way is south. If south is directly ahead of you, then your garden is south facing. A south-facing garden will have little shade, while a north-facing one is likely to be in shade for much of the day.

Other factors, such as nearby buildings, trees and high hedges, can increase the shade in certain areas. Shade also changes through the day, as the sun moves around your garden. It changes through the year too – when the sun is high in the sky in summer, the shadows cast are quite short, but in winter the sun barely rises above the horizon and shadows are long.

When do you like to sit in the sunshine – morning or evening? If that refreshing sundowner is the highlight of the day, any seating or patio area needs to be positioned where it will catch the evening rays, unless you're a shade lover. If there's room, have more than one seating area, including at least one for a table and chairs. And remember that chairs need to be pulled out from a table in order to sit round it, so make sure the patio is large enough for that.

Any unshaded beds and borders will make a good home for bright-flowered plants such as summer bedding and the majority of flowering shrubs. Shady areas can be planted up with hostas, ferns and other lovers of low light levels. Planting areas facing north or east will receive less direct sun than those facing south or west – match the plants to the situation and you'll find they grow far better.

So before you decide to plant anything, go outside and take a look at exactly how much sunlight your garden gets during the day and at which times.

Actions:
– Check which way your garden faces
– Decide where you want your seating areas

Right: Take time to assess your garden before taking any action

How much shade does your garden have?

If south is directly ahead of you, then your garden is south-facing – which means that you will have plenty of sun shining towards the back of the house. In this scenario the boundary at the end of your garden is north-facing, and so it will be pretty much in shade all day. The left-hand fence will be on the eastern side and so is west facing, receiving the afternoon and evening sun. The right-hand fence or wall is, therefore, your west fence, which is east facing and will get some morning sun. For clarity, draw a rectangle on a piece of paper and, once you know where south is, mark it on and fill in all the gaps.

SOUTH FACING

You'll have little shade and lots of sun shining onto the back of the house. The far boundary faces north, so will be pretty much in shade all day. If you stand with your back to the house, your right-hand boundary will be east facing and get morning sun, while your left-hand one will face west and get afternoon and evening sun.

Planting tips: Climbers for the north-facing boundary include *Parthenocissus henryana*, *Hydrangea petiolaris* and ivies of all kinds, or try shade-tolerant wall shrubs such as *chaenomeles* and witch hazel. For foliage, add ferns and hostas, and for flowers plant daphne, brunnera and fragrant lily of the valley.

Below: Plants such as ferns and hydrangeas will thrive in partial shade

NORTH FACING

This garden will have areas of shade for much of the day; however, even a north-facing surface (such as the back wall of the house) won't always be in full shade – it's surprising how much evening sun it will get between May and October. All but the most heat-loving plants enjoy a bit of midday shelter from the sun, which also stops pale colours burning out.

Planting tips: Try woodlanders such as hellebores, snowdrops and pulmonaria, which flower early, before the tree canopy shades out the light, and put on growth through summer despite the shade overhead. They're ideal for areas that only get early morning sun.

EAST FACING

An east-facing garden gets most of its sun during the morning. Plants that like partial shade and need shelter from strong sunlight will thrive in this garden. Afternoon shade protects plants from the sun at its hottest. Evening shade will enhance the impact of white flowers that attract pollinating moths, rather than butterflies, and are often exceptionally fragrant too.

Below: Hellebores and snowdrops brighten areas beneath deciduous trees in early spring

Planting tips: White-flowered *Nicotiana sylvestris* likes evening shade and brings rich fragrance too. Plants that cope with morning sun and cool conditions include the flowering climbers *Clematis alpina* and honeysuckle (*Lonicera*), and shrubs such as berberis.

WEST FACING

West-facing gardens are in shade in the morning and get sun during the afternoon and evening. In winter, morning shade is a protective shroud for plants such as camellias. If their flowers get frosted overnight, bright morning sun can thaw them out too fast, bursting their cells and causing the petals to turn brown. Plants in a west-facing garden or area must also be able to withstand the heat of the afternoon sun during the summer months.

Planting tips: Trees and shrubs that will suit these conditions include magnolias and camellias, which like the morning shade, and perennials such as sedums and fuchsias.

Below: Camellias flourish in west-facing borders that get morning shade

What type of shade is it?

Choosing plants that will thrive in your borders depends upon knowing the conditions they will be growing in. If you have patches of shade in your garden, it's important to work out what type of shade it is.

DEEP SHADE
Found under evergreen trees, on the north side of walls or in the shadow of buildings. These areas tend to be cold and dry. Choose shade-loving, not just shade-tolerant, plants such as leafy ferns, hostas and ivy, and flowering daphnes and lily of the valley.

PARTIAL SHADE
Most gardens have areas that get sun for only part of the day – between three and six hours in summer – depending on their aspect, as the sun moves across the sky. Which part of the day your area is in shade makes a difference. Alchemilla and hardy geraniums relish partial shade.

DAPPLED SHADE
This is common under deciduous trees. Dappled shade all day is equal to three hours of summer sun. In summer, when in full leaf, trees cast a patchwork of shade, but from autumn to spring let in full sun. This is ideal for woodland plants such as anemones and primulas that flower in the spring sunshine before trees come into leaf.

TOP TIP

The prevailing wind in the UK is usually from the south west, so if your garden is exposed, consider planting a hedge on that side of the garden to filter strong winds. On really exposed sites and in coastal areas, it makes sense to establish a hedge as a windbreak, before planting up areas with expensive trees and shrubs. Strong winds not only blow plants over, but they also dry them out and cause wind burn. Get the hedge established first and its filtering effect will save you much heartache.

What kind of soil do you have?

Have a dig around to see what type of soil you are dealing with. If your soil is gritty and not sticky, it's likely a free-draining sandy soil and Mediterranean plants are the order of the day. If your soil is heavy and very sticky when wet, then it's likely to be clay, and roses and hardy geraniums will thrive. Many soils will be somewhere in between, which allows you to grow a wide range of plants.

Understanding the soil in your garden is extremely important and will ultimately determine the plants you can grow. If you have different areas of good and poor soil this may also be a key factor in deciding the overall layout of your garden. You will, of course, want to make sure the main planting areas use the good soil and that hard landscaping areas – which will work whatever the soil is like underneath – are sited on the poorer areas. Depending on the size of your garden, it's worth checking the soil from different parts of the plot, rather than just one area, as it can vary enormously.

Right: Add a layer of organic matter to your soil to improve its structure

WHAT'S THE TEXTURE?

Sandy or gravelly soil will feel gritty when it is run through your fingers and dries out rapidly after rainfall, making cultivation easy. But it quickly loses nutrients, so adding bulky organic matter regularly is vital to hold on to both water and nutrients.

Clay soil binds together in clods when dry, and when it is wet it will reveal a polished surface when rubbed. Squeeze it into a ball and it will remain tight. It is fertile and retains water. Clay with flints is particularly hard to cultivate.

Loam – every gardener's ideal – has a moderate clay content so that when it is damp it will hold together when squeezed into a ball, but the ball can be easily crumbled and broken apart.

Peaty soils from the fens tend to be dark, almost black, and will be springy when squeezed. Adding sharp sand and grit improves their drainage.

TOP TIP

An easy way to test drainage is to get a watering can and water an area of soil. If the surface water disappears quickly, you're probably on a sandy or gravelly soil, but if it sits for a while, you're probably on clay.

ACID OR ALKALINE?

A simple soil testing kit will tell you how acid or alkaline your soil is. Acid soil has a pH reading below 7 (neutral) and alkaline soil a pH reading above 7. On chalky or limestone soils, which are alkaline, you won't be able to grow lime-haters such as rhododendrons and camellias (except in pots of ericaceous – lime-free – compost) – their leaves will turn yellow and they'll become sickly. But there are plenty of other plants that love alkaline soil, from clematis to hardy geraniums, dianthus to peonies. Growing plants that are happy at your pH level will save you hours of pandering to their whims when they're out of sorts.

If you don't have the right type of soil for the plants you want to grow, raised beds are a good option. You can then import topsoil to suit the plants you want to grow, and if bending down and mobility are an issue, they can be a real boon. Make them from stone, brick or wooden sleepers. They're usually between 45cm and 60cm high.

Testing the soil in our gardens is vital if we want to know which plants will do well and which ones will struggle, thus avoiding wasting money.

HOW TO TEST YOUR SOIL

🕐 15 MINUTE TASK
BEST TIME TO DO: YEAR ROUND

1. Collect small soil samples from the part of your garden you wish to test. Bear in mind that the pH may vary slightly across the garden (though seldom extremely).

2. Dry the soil near a radiator or other heat source and remove any stones or debris that could skew the reading. Mix up the soil samples and add to a test tube.

3. Pour the indicator fluid in the quantity suggested – usually up to a line marked on the test tube.

This fluid is specially formulated to detect the soil's acidity or alkalinity.

4. Shake the soil and fluid for half a minute, then let the mixture settle to reveal the colour of the fluid. Check this against the chart to find out its pH value.

INDICATOR PLANTS
Alkaline – clematis, dianthus, honeysuckle, spindle
Acid – azalea, rhododendron, pieris, blue hydrangea

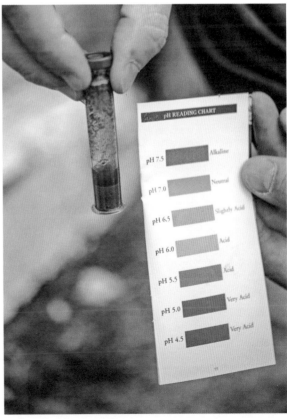

Simple ways to improve your soil

Look upon soil improvement as something ongoing rather than an emergency measure. Don't think that one initial go at improving your soil is enough.

Organic matter (such as garden compost or well-rotted manure) will bind together a thin, sandy soil and open up a clay soil. But organic matter rots down and disappears over time, so apply it every spring as a mulch – spread well-rotted manure or homemade compost over the soil surface around your plants in a layer about 5cm thick. It'll do wonders for their growth, for soil moisture retention and for deterring weeds.

Also add a good dusting (two or three clenched fistfuls to the square metre) of blood, fish and bonemeal in March or April – before the mulch – to give your plants a boost. Then repeat in June, just before a shower is forecast.

SOIL DOS

○ Pick up a handful of soil and feel it from time to time, to work out whether it would benefit from the addition of more organic matter or grit, depending on its nature.

○ Add bulky organic matter to the vegetable plot each winter if you're digging.

○ Mulch beds and borders with organic matter in spring, where digging the soil over is undesirable and unnecessary. Mulching will help conserve moisture and keep down weeds.

○ Use organic fertilisers that are more beneficial to soil bacteria than inorganic compounds, and be sure to water them in.

○ Consider growing green manures on the veg patch – these are seedling crops that are dug back in to add enrichment.

SOIL DON'TS

○ Don't underestimate the value of sharp grit and coarse sand in improving the drainage of heavy clay.

○ Never apply fresh manure to soil. This can reduce the amount of nitrogen available to your plants, because bacteria use nitrogen in the process of breaking down the manure.

○ Don't dig heavy clay when it is too wet (sticky) or too dry (rock hard). Wait for that quarter of an hour in spring when it is somewhere between the two!

○ Don't dig just for the sake of it. Once planted, the ground can be enriched by mulching and allowing worms to help incorporate it.

○ Don't apply products whose value you are unsure about. Soil is a precious commodity and should be cherished.

Spring

(MARCH TO MAY)

This is a busy time of year in the garden. The soil is warming up, new growth is emerging and there's a long list of gardening jobs to do. It's also an exciting time, a season to sow veg and flower seeds, start mowing the lawn and plant summer flowering bulbs.

- Sow annual plants such as cosmos and tender vegetable crops like beans and courgettes on the windowsill.

- Finish any winter pruning such as late clematis, roses and late-flowering shrubs

- Prick out and pot on plants grown from seed as they develop.

- Plant summer-flowering bulbs such as alliums and gladioli in pots and borders.

- Sow edible crops such as lettuce, carrots and radish directly outside from mid-spring.

- Sow tender veg such as sweetcorn directly outside and plant up pots and hanging baskets when frosts have passed. Sow herbs such as coriander and basil outside.

- Plant early potatoes

- Start to mow lawns once a week.

- Nip out weeds as you spot them.

- Be vigilant and on the lookout for pests and diseases on plants.

- Water plants when necessary.

- Stake taller plants as they grow.

- Give shrubs, herbaceous plants and climbers a general slow-release feed and mulch.

- Put out large pots and water butts to collect rainwater.

Summer

(JUNE TO AUGUST)

Enjoy your garden at its best as your borders fill with flowers and veg beds begin to yield harvests. Keep on top of tasks like deadheading and watering to keep plants healthy and looking their best.

○ Check plants to see if they need water every day.

○ Prune early flowering shrubs.

○ Look out for pest and disease problems.

○ Keep on hoeing and digging out weeds in beds and borders.

○ Mow lawns at least once a week.

○ Deadhead flowering plants by removing all faded blooms to encourage further flowering.

○ Plant out tender plants.

○ Trim topiary.

○ Continue to sow salad crops early in the season.

○ Feed fruiting edible crops, such as tomatoes, as well as hanging baskets and pots planted with summer bedding, every couple of weeks with a high-potash liquid feed.

○ Harvest edible plants such as beans and raspberries regularly to keep crops coming.

○ Plant strawberries in pots, growing bags or in the ground at the end of the season.

○ Plant autumn flowering bulbs.

Autumn

(SEPTEMBER TO NOVEMBER)

The growing season is coming to a close, but there is still plenty to do, from trimming evergreen hedges to harvesting the last of the tomatoes and taking cuttings. This is also a good time of year to plant trees and shrubs, while the ground is still warm.

○ Plant pots with winter-flowering plants such as pansies and viburnum.

○ Trim evergreen hedges

○ Plant new trees and shrubs when they are dormant.

○ Plant out spring-flowering bulbs.

○ Keep harvesting fruit and veg until the frosts or plants are spent.

○ Clear away finished summer bedding and spent edible plants and add to your compost heap.

○ Sow sweet peas on the windowsill for next spring.

○ Plant and sow overwintering broad beans, onions and peas outside.

○ Tidy up plants to stop pests and diseases overwintering.

○ Remove dead leaves and cut back perennials that don't have hollow stems or interesting seedheads that wildlife can use in winter.

○ Rake up leaves and compost them.

○ Bring pots of tender plants such as pelargoniums inside before the frosts strike, or protect with fleece.

○ Prune autumn raspberries.

○ Collect leaves to make leafmould.

○ Put out food for the birds.

Winter

(DECEMBER TO FEBRUARY)

Winter is the time to prune fruit trees, clean your tools and pots, and get things in order before the spring. Put out food for the birds and crack the ice in bird baths and ponds, to help wildlife.

○ Shake the snow from plants to prevent damage.

○ Turn compost to speed up decomposition.

○ Start sowing edible crops that will need a long growing season, such as aubergines, tomatoes and chillies, on the windowsill towards the end of the season.

○ Prune fruit trees and bushes (apart from stone fruits).

○ Chit seed potatoes in late winter (February) by placing them in trays on a windowsill before planting in early spring (see page 158).

○ Prune deciduous shrubs that are pruned in the dormant season, such as roses.

○ Plant out deciduous trees and shrubs in the garden or in large containers.

○ Deadhead and tidy up winter displays in pots and containers.

○ Put out food and water for birds to help them through the barren winter months.

○ Start planning what to grow and where for the new gardening year ahead.

Jargon buster

Aspect – the direction in which a garden faces (north, south etc.).

Ericaceous – describing plants such as blueberries or azaleas that need acidic soil, or the compost that these plants need to grow in.

Mulching – adding a layer to conserve moisture in the soil and suppress weeds: it could be made up of shredded bark, compost, pebbles, etc.

Organic matter – this usually refers to well-rotted manure, compost or leafmould that can be mixed into the soil or placed on the surface to improve it.

Topsoil – this is the upper layer of soil (a layer of around 30cm), which should be full of organic matter and nutrients. You can buy this to add to your borders.

CHAPTER TWO

Get the balance right

Get the balance right

Left: Paving and a limited colour scheme creates a contemporary look

Whether you have a blank canvas or already have borders in place, making changes can be intimidating – but they can also be very rewarding. So if your garden doesn't suit your needs, has become tired or too familiar and no longer fills you with joy, then set about making it lift your spirits. The last few years have taught us a lot about the value of our outdoor space and the benefits of fresh air and contact with nature when it comes to improving our mental health. So it's important to make the most of your garden and ensure it works well for you. Even minor changes will make a huge difference.

Do bear in mind that you're bound to make some mistakes along the way – we all do – but remember that nothing is set in stone (except an expensive patio!). Plants that have been put in the wrong place will soon become apparent and can easily be moved.

Lists are useful. Write down the things you really want, so your garden will enrich your life: a place to sit, somewhere to entertain, space to grow veg, fruit or fragrant flowers, a shed, a greenhouse . . .

Look at the path of the sun – especially in winter. Do you want your morning coffee or your evening tipple in the sun? That, at least, will begin to give you an idea of what you need to put where. Prioritise your changes and tackle them in phases – hard landscaping (paths and patios) first, planting second. That way both your nerves and your bank balance stand a chance of surviving.

Doing the job yourself is obviously the least expensive approach, but if you don't feel confident about the more elaborate operations, ask others who have gardens you admire for advice. They will always share their views on what worked and what didn't. Never be afraid to admit your limitations. If your plans include adding electrics, always call in a qualified electrician.

You will need a master plan: a view of what you're aiming for. You don't have to do it all at once, unless you have the time and money. If you know where you're going and tackle the job a little at a time, you'll be encouraged by your small gains. Joined together they will make a huge difference.

Core skills:
– Drawing a garden plan

5 steps to success

1. **Look at the views** from your windows – the kitchen especially – and assess if your current garden looks good from the most frequented spots. Whether your garden is old or new, analyse what you don't like about it and set about making amends. Can you see it all in one go? If that's the case, start off by creating a journey through it – even if the garden is tiny, it can still be divided up with small internal hedges or taller shrubs so you are tempted to explore and find hidden nooks that are lovely to sit in.

2. **Plot your essentials** – such as somewhere to sit, a path that is even – and interesting – to traverse, and screening from neighbours. But be considerate when it comes to fence height – 2m will give you privacy without robbing your neighbours of too much light.

3. **Make beds as deep and wide as you can** and plant relatively closely in soil that has been enriched with organic matter. Not only will the plants grow better, they will also cover the ground faster and leave little room for weeds.

4. **Think vertically** as well as horizontally – use arches, wigwams and pergolas to lift up your display wherever a tree would be too large or too dominant.

5. **Include focal points** – objects or small trees will draw you in and make you want to explore. Push canes into the ground to mark their possible positions and use trails of sand on the ground to mark out where you'd like beds. Leave them there for a few days while you eye them up and walk around, imagining what they'll be like. Aim for a design that is interesting but simple – and avoid too many different hard landscaping materials. As a rule of thumb, three different kinds is a maximum. Any more than that and your garden will start to look bitty and overly busy.

Right: Deep, plant-packed borders are popular in cottage gardens

Right: Decking provides a place to relax and enjoy the view of your garden

Above: Using light paving stones can make a garden look bigger

Left: Rectangular pieces of wood, set at an angle make an eye-catching path

How much landscaping do you need?

Unlike painting a picture, where the frame is chosen once the artistry is complete, a garden is created the other way round: the frame (the hard landscaping) is constructed first, then the picture (the planting) is positioned within it.

If you want a garden rather than an installation, aim for a ratio of two-thirds planting to one-third hard landscaping (paving and the like). If you're a minimalist, you may want to adjust this, but when hard landscaping is dominant the overall effect is sleeker and more architectural but less relaxed in style.

Plants can be used to mask fences and blur the hard edges of a path or terrace, if that's the effect you want. Much depends on taste here. If you only rent your property, you can rely on containers for structure, as they can go with you when you move. Hard landscaping is expensive and would have to stay.

And plastic grass? Perhaps on tiny patches for little kids' games of football. Elsewhere paving, gravel, chipped bark, rolled hoggin and groundcover planting will do the same job and are (mostly!) infinitely more environmentally friendly.

How much should I tackle myself?

Left: Pergolas provide an attractive structure to cover with a mix of climbers

If you want to save money there are many jobs you can tackle yourself. Other jobs are best left to the professionals. Here's a guide:

DIY JOBS:

○ **Planting a tree** or large shrub – choose the spot wisely and prepare the soil well.

○ **Enlarging a border** or making a new one – draw up a planting plan, taking note of positioning and numbers of plants needed.

○ **Installing a small pond** – make it at least 2m long and 1.5m wide and use underlay and a proper liner. Take care to mask the edges well, for a professional finish.

○ **Painting fences** – choose your colour carefully. Bright colours will quickly pale, softer shades less so, and dark colours will merge into the background.

○ **Putting up an arch** or pergola – but do make sure the posts are firmly anchored in the ground. Climbers can get very heavy!

BEST LEFT TO THE PROFESSIONALS:

○ **Installing mains electrical equipment** such as garden lighting. Connecting up a pump in a pond may well be within your abilities, but don't risk larger jobs.

○ **Laying a patio** or a large and complex path – foundations and levels are important and unless you know how to manage them, give in!

○ **Installing drainage** – strenuous and complicated in terms of falls and soakaways. Let someone else take the strain.

○ **Erecting a greenhouse** – you'll crack more panes than you would have believed possible, unless you have a skilled helpmate.

○ **Putting up fencing** – it's a heavy job and not for the faint hearted. The posts should be durable (not softwood) and well anchored.

What to include in your design

Consider which elements you would like or need, how you would use them and the styles you prefer.

TERRACES AND PATIOS

These are transitions between the house and garden, so having a strong link with the building can really start to set the tone for the garden. This area is also normally the first viewing platform and social space, so the size and shape is very important. The terrace should feel comfortable, with a good balance of hard materials and softer planting.

FEATURES

Use pots, sculptures and furniture to really personalise your garden. They should be elements that catch your eye and are probably something that should be added over a period of time and not rushed.

STEPS AND LEVELS

Changes in level can create interesting viewpoints, but also a sense of comfort. Providing a sunken space, even in a small garden, can really hunker you down into the landscape. Making steps wider than they need to be at the front door can make the entrance feel more welcoming. Flip it the other way and reduce the width of the steps between spaces to create a sense of tension and surprise.

STRUCTURES

Great for bringing a vertical element to your design quickly, these can be useful focal points and supports for climbers. Arbours, arches and obelisks, along with practical structures like sheds and greenhouses, all provide additional year-round interest. To work well, they must have a real purpose and sit comfortably within the space.

WATER

This is a great addition to any garden, and can be introduced in various ways. Consider what you want – movement or reflective stillness, gentle or refreshing sounds, informal or formal style, more wildlife?

PATHS

These are one of the most important elements, as they can guide our movement and help us engage with the space. They're not just practical either – they can play a big visual role, drawing the eye around the garden and helping to control the speed at which we move through the space.

BOUNDARIES

Walls, fences and hedges form the backdrop to your whole garden, so your choice of colours, materials, and textures is really important. The best gardens, whatever their size, all deal with their boundaries really well.

Simplify curves around the edge of a lawn to make mowing easy and give a clean, smooth line to a border.

Use simple shapes such as geometric circles and squares for lawns and paved areas as a good starting point, and don't forget to plan in functional features at this stage, such as paths, bin stores, washing lines and compost heaps, as well as sheds and greenhouses.

Graduate the height of plants to create a bank of foliage and flowers that will help to frame the view of your garden and soften the stark angles created between ground level and fences or walls.

Create a sense of space in gardens with large, rectangular lawns bordered by narrow flowerbeds, by cutting off the corners to form deeper beds that provide a contrast to the rectangular shape.

Break up the space

It might seem odd to divide a small space into even smaller areas, but it is a classic trick designers use to make an area look and feel bigger. Not being able to see the whole garden at once makes it difficult to quantify a space, and hiding even just a corner from view with a cleverly placed container or large shrub is enough to make us want to see more, and believe that there is something else to come, just out of sight.

Make seating more useful
Having somewhere to sit and relax in the garden is a vital feature for most of us, but when space is lacking even the furniture needs to multi-task. Use benches or box seating that can double up as tool storage or a space to keep children's toys. Or make the edges to raised beds high enough and wide enough so they can also be comfortable spots to perch – add cushions to complete your seat.

Make the most of pots

If you want to include containers, it's best to have a small number of large ones, to create greater dramatic effect. Large pots also dry out less quickly on hot days, so you won't have to become a slave to the hosepipe. Install a drip irrigation system for pots if you lead a busy life.

Reflect the light

A well-placed mirror will make your space feel bigger and brighter instantly. Help it blend in by planting around the base and edges, and angle it so that it reflects planting or a water feature rather than a wall or path. Opt for an aged or mottled mirror that will create less distinct reflections, giving the illusion of space but avoiding the risk of birds flying into it. Choose a mirror where the glass is partially obscured to further reduce the risk.

Bring into focus

A good design draws the eye into the garden and leads you to points that the designer wants you to look at. A focal point can be a key feature around which the design radiates or something that draws you down a path and invites you to explore. It doesn't need to be grand or expensive – a well-placed pot, bench, small tree or graceful shrub will do the job.

Add lighting

Adding lighting to your garden can enhance areas of planting, trees, focal points or water features. The great thing about the garden at night is you can light up the best bits and hide unattractive things that are harder to cover up during the day.

Look up

Using height in a small space leads the eye upwards and helps to expand our view of the garden and make it feel larger. In a small garden, the temptation is to restrict yourself to small plants, but this can make the garden feel cluttered. A strategically placed tree or tall shrub, obelisk, statue or structure such as an arch will help to break up a space into different areas to make it feel bigger.

Less is more

If you love plants then you may be tempted to shoehorn as many varieties as possible into your plot. This can result in a 'spotty' and disjointed look. Instead, try limiting the colour scheme of your plants, and then carrying it through to furniture colours and wall or fence finishes.

Grow up walls

Clothing vertical spaces, such as walls and fences, in plants will increase your growing area without taking up too much space on the ground. They will also help soften hard edges, blending them with the surroundings. Climbers are the easiest way to do this, with trellis or horizontal wires stretched across your wall or fence to train them onto. A scented climber, such as this star jasmine, is within sniffing distance next to a seat (right).

Year-round appeal

Foliage plants are some of the best value, hardest working plants in any garden and can have a huge impact on the look – it's no surprise they feature prominently at flower shows.

Ajuga (below) offers intensely coloured ground cover, while clipped topiary forms of box and yew provide strong, year-round structure that is the ideal foil for the filigree foliage of acers.

Focus on: small gardens

BRIGHTEN UP HARD SURFACES

Small gardens, especially in towns and cities, are often shaded by buildings, boundaries and trees so can be dark, gloomy spaces. Using light-toned materials wherever possible can make a huge difference, lifting the space and making it more inviting.

Bounce the available light around the garden by using light paving, pale gravel mulch over dark soil, and painting or staining the boundaries a light colour. Not only will this make the space seem bigger, but it will also show your plants off to their best advantage.

DIVIDE UP YOUR SPACE

Even the smallest plot will seem bigger if you can't see everything immediately. Dividing the garden with hedges, internal walls or screens covered in climbers feels like a strange thing to do when space is tight, but this approach creates a sense of intrigue and brings a feeling of going on a journey. By introducing hidden corners and giving each area a distinct style or atmosphere, the garden will make an impact way beyond its size.

KEEP THE LAYOUT SIMPLE

Less is definitely more when it comes to small gardens. Trying to cram too much stuff and too many different ideas into a small space can make it look crowded and fussy. When working on small gardens, it's best to keep the design very simple in its layout and focus, and the planting and colour palette limited and homogeneous. The result will be a smart and unified design that is attractive and restful on the eye.

MAKE SEATING WORK HARDER

Furniture is often treated as an afterthought or simply a finishing touch, but when space is limited it should be an integral part of your garden, and should be practical as well as attractive. Consider building seating into a garden – capping a retaining wall with a nice piece of timber or making a bench double up as storage. When making your own seating, aim for a height of around 45cm and choose materials that will complement the plants and landscaping around it.

Right: Simple planting creates a calm atmosphere in a small garden

PICK PLANTS FOR LONGER INTEREST

Plants must earn their keep in confined spaces. You need key plants with poise and stature, which will look good through several seasons. Small acers, spindle trees (*Euonymus alatus*) and *Clerodendrum trichotomum* are all great. Look for tall, elegant shrubs that will be bursting with flowers early in the year, followed by boughs of berries and vibrant autumn foliage. Extend the interest with underplanting – shuttlecock ferns are great for providing greenery through several seasons and daffodils will brighten the base in spring. Use your shrub as a climbing frame for a clematis to give a summer boost and add cyclamen around it for late-season colour.

LIMIT YOUR COLOUR PALETTE

You can have too much of a good thing. Gardeners love colourful plants, and lots of them, but by showing a little restraint we can make our gardens appear larger and more cohesive. This doesn't mean denying ourselves colour, it just means using it more carefully, planting larger groups of plants of the same colour to create greater impact. Too many plants of too small a number with too much variation can lead to a dotty 'pizza' effect.

USE FEWER AND LARGER PLANTS

Remember you're making a small garden, not a garden for small people. Too many little plants make a space look fussy. Select big plants that have architectural value and impact. *Rhamnus alaternus*, ceanothus, eriobotrya and pittosporum all provide height and impact. Train them up a wall or shape into trees. They will obscure boundaries and make the space feel bigger.

PLANT UP YOUR BOUNDARIES

You've filled the borders, crammed every container and still your urge to grow new plants is unsatisfied. Don't despair, go upwards. We all have boundaries to our gardens: fences, walls and hedges are all valuable growing spaces. Cover them in climbers, such as roses and clematis. But also try something different: scramble *Tropaeolum speciosum* through hedges or grow espaliered peaches or apricots against a wall.

DITCH THE LAWN

A lawn can accentuate the smallness of little gardens. Turning it into a gravel garden provides scope for imaginative planting that will tease and hold the eye, creating interest and a sense that the space is larger than it is. Gravel is a wonderful medium for plants. It allows you to engage with and walk among them in a more intimate way than just admiring your hard work from one side of a bed.

HOW TO MAKE A GARDEN PLAN

WEEKEND TASK
BEST TIME TO DO: ANY TIME

You will need:
– pencil
– notebook
– measuring tape
– paper (A1 or A2 size is best)
– tracing paper

Before you can start designing, you need to measure your garden and draw up a simple plan to scale. This may feel like a lot of work, but it'll save time and money in the long run. You wouldn't buy a kitchen or bathroom without measuring up, and it's no different with a garden.

1. Start by drawing a rough sketch of your garden, noting the house (including windows, doors, taps, etc.), along with trees, sheds, borders and drains – in fact, anything that may be included in or affect the design.

2. Take the basic measurements to enable you to draw your plan to scale. Measure where doors and windows sit in your house, the length of the boundaries, and where specific existing elements, such as trees, sheds and patios, sit in the plot.

3. Make a note of any changes in level, particularly around your house. If you have lots of complicated levels, it may be worth hiring a laser level from your local hire centre. They're easy to use, but you'll also find tips online if you need them.

4. Draw up your final scaled plan of the current garden, using a compass to check orientation. You may like to work on paper, drawing it as if you're looking out from the house, as that is your everyday connection with the garden. Use the biggest piece of paper you can (A1 or A2) – the larger your plan, the easier it is to understand your space. A scale of 1:50 (2cm on your page equals 1m in your garden) or 1:100 (1cm on your plan equals 1m in your garden).

5. Once your survey is drawn up, place the tracing paper over the top to start drawing up your design – this way you only need one copy of your scaled plan. When you first put pencil to paper to start design, it may feel strange. But just take your time and don't try to get to the finished garden too quickly. Initially, avoid getting hung up on specifics. Play with shapes and ideas. Imagine yourself in different areas. How it will feel there and what will you be looking at? You don't want to create a lovely seating area that faces the bins! Imagine moving through it and consider if you can add a little element of surprise here and there – perhaps the sound of running water?

If you have trouble understanding it on paper, pop outside and mark things out with canes. This will help you visualise how your ideas are working in the space, and allow you to check the views – both good and bad.

Initially, focus on simple shapes rather than specific plants and avoid getting bogged down in detail. As you build your layers, think in groups of plants, not in ones or twos. Plants in nature grow in clusters, with a few single plants set a short distance away. Mimic this to get a sense of flow and rhythm with your planting. Once you're happy with the overall shape of the planting, use the following steps to work on the specifics, but don't rush it. Try several versions, laying new pieces of tracing paper over your drawing until you're happy with the result. As you apply plant names to the shapes and forms, revise the details, looking at the contrast between the foliage, sizes and textures.

A. Start by placing trees (or working with the ones already in your garden), thinking about how their shape will affect the light and work with the wider landscape and buildings.

B. Position the shrubs. These counterbalance the trees and bring that upper level down into the garden. Add different shapes and forms, some more solid, others relaxed and open.

C. Include perennials. Remember to think in groups, keeping rhythm and repetition in mind.

D. Add annual plants, bulbs and corms, considering where they will provide little highlights.

TOP TIP
For the greatest impact, group single-colour flowers together rather than a mix of colours.

DESIGN DOS

○ Remember that space is more important than clutter. Just like the silences in music, spaces show off what surrounds them.

○ Patios and terraces need to be large enough to allow chairs to be pulled away from the table without falling off the edge.

○ Make new borders big enough to be useful – a bed can look large on a plan, but in reality, there may not be space for more than one or two plants.

○ Increase the depth or width of borders, so you can include a variety of plants of different shapes and heights to give an illusion of space and help screen boundaries.

○ Reduce the number of small beds and borders, combining them together or turfing over to integrate into the lawn.

DESIGN DON'TS

○ Don't be afraid of colour, but have at least some corners of your garden that are calm rather than frantic.

○ Resist the temptation to cram too many decorative features into your garden. Better to have one good big feature, such as a pond, rather than a sprinkle of water features and arbours.

○ Avoid 'pinch' points, where flowerbeds taper down and become too narrow for any worthwhile planting and can often end up as bare soil.

Actions:
– Make a list of the features you want in your garden
– Draw a garden plan

CHAPTER THREE

Right plant, right place

Right plant, right place

The ideal garden is one which has something of interest all the year round (granted, in June and July this is easier to achieve than in November), one which has form and stature as well as colour, and one in which the plants are growing happily thanks in part to your soil and situation, but also to your ability to offer them a bit of TLC.

The plants you choose will affect the whole mood of the garden, and although this can vary depending on the part of the country where you live – how warm, how cold, how sheltered or how windy it is, coupled with the prevailing soil conditions – the approach to planting is the same the world over: start with the big stuff and work your way downwards.

Construct your garden's planting scheme as if you were creating a human body. Yes, you may not be Dr Frankenstein, but this approach offers a good way of remembering that the bones that form the skeleton come first (trees and large shrubs), followed by the flesh (smaller plants and evergreens to offer year-round form), and the features (the colourful, seasonal plants) which are usually smaller, come last.

Even small gardens need plants to give height, to avoid them looking like what the great gardener Beth Chatto used to call 'a tray of scones'. Verticals in the form of trees (even small ones) and climbing plants trained up obelisks and tripods will encourage you to look up and will give the garden that vital third dimension. So . . . trees first. But how many? Enough to lift your scheme but not to envelop the garden in shade. In a small garden two or three small trees will be ample – things like silver birches, which have a feathery canopy, or crab apples. Another choice would be the Tibetan cherry, *Prunus serrula*, with glossy mahogany-coloured bark that gleams in low winter sunshine, offering interest when other trees are bare and skeletal – though even then they will offer welcome stature. Allow for their spread after ten years or so, making sure that sunlight will still penetrate between them for the plants that grow below.

TOP TIP

Plan in layers – think of your garden as though it were an elegant three- or even four-storey country house. Planting in layers is a recipe for success if you get it right, with the trees spreading their canopy as the upper storey, the shrubs and evergreens below, followed by the ground-floor planting of perennials and the basement of ground-huggers.

Before you splash out on trees, look at the gardens around you to see what does well. If there are no rhododendrons and camellias in your locale you probably have alkaline – chalky – soil and they will not be happy growing direct into the earth. If you adore them and simply must have them you will have to grow them in containers of ericaceous (lime-free) compost.

Get out into the garden and use canes to mark the potential spots for trees. Stand back and eye them up from various places, including inside the house, both upstairs and down. When you are satisfied that you have the right positions, make your choice and plant them before anything else. Shrubs come next. When you are first planning out a bed, think in terms of triangles – both vertical and horizontal. Broad or narrow pyramid shapes of tiered planting are pleasing to the eye. In general, taller plants are best at the back of a bed or border and shorter ones at the front. It stands to reason that if you do it the other way round you won't see the lower-growing ones behind those that are taller. That said, it's interesting to have a few 'ribs' of taller planting stretching in descending order of height to the front of the border from the back, so that as you walk along it there are 'bays' where more plants come into view.

Don't be too 'dotty' with your placement of shrubs. Plant three or four of them in relatively close proximity (allowing for growth) and leave triangular swathes of earth between them to plant perennials and ground-cover plants.

Be aware that some plants insist on being in full sun and others prefer to be in some shade. Aim to choose the right plant for the right place – ferns, hostas and other green things are happy in shade, while most bright flowers love sun.

Evergreen plants, including topiary specimens – yew clipped into orbs and pyramids for instance – will offer year-round form. Use them as focal points and try to get the balance right. Too many evergreens and the garden will remain static for most of the year; too few and its form and stature will evaporate in winter.

And remember, anything that turns out to be in the wrong place can always be moved to another position. It's easy to panic about planting schemes, but they are not set in stone and often need adjusting even in the best-regulated of gardens.

When it comes to the rest of the plants in your garden, by all means grow what you like, but bear in mind that a bed or border with larger numbers of fewer varieties of plant will always look more cohesive and less dotty. In other words, if you can fit in 50 plants, ten each of five varieties will have more impact than five each of ten varieties. (If you love plants this is often a hard decision to make.) The choice is personal to you.

In terms of foliage, choose some plants with bold, unfussy leaves as well as some that are frothy and ethereal. Your eye will enjoy the difference in textures.

Plant thickly, allowing room for plants to fill out, but not so far apart that you must gaze on a sea of earth between them for months until they are established. As a rule of thumb, plant perennials at a spacing of about 30cm, shrubs at about a metre. Yes, you might have to thin them out after a few years, but you can always use the thinnings elsewhere or give them away to friends.

Core skills:
– Plant research
– Learning about types of plants
– Planting bulbs
– Combining plants

5 steps to success

(1) **Check plants sizes before buying.** It's easy to be optimistic about all your plants fitting into your border when you are looking at a shrub in a two-litre pot, but make sure you check its eventual height and spread. When planting you'll need to leave room for plants to grow, or in two or three years' time you may find yourself having to move everything around. However, it's also worth researching how fast growing each plant is. Some trees or shrubs may take more than ten years to reach their eventual height.

(2) **Plan ahead.** In gardening you need to think about what you need to do this season to prepare for the next. For example, if you plant spring-flowering bulbs in autumn you can have colour from January through to June. You might want to order roses in the summer in order to plant them in the autumn, when they will establish well. This type of forward planning will give you something to look forward to and help create a garden where there's always something to enjoy.

(3) **Include year round interest.** Think beyond summer and include plants that will give you something to look at year round. Use evergreen shrubs to add interest in winter. Include early spring-flowering bulbs, trees that have three seasons of interest and plants that flower for longer than a few weeks. Even in a small garden, it's possible to have something to look at year round if you include a mix of evergreen shrubs, winter and summer-flowering clematis and long-flowering perennials.

(4) **Go with the flow.** Following natural rules is the only way to garden. Fighting nature or trying to control it by forcing plants to do something they can't is not only pointless but counterproductive. If your soil is alkaline, why struggle to grow rhododendrons? There are so many plants for every soil and situation. Going with the flow is so much easier and it's gratifying to see plants in their element, enjoying life and developing to their true potential, rather than putting up a brave fight and struggling to survive.

(5) **Know what is where.** Remember what you've planted where, either by using labels or noting it down. Many bulbs disappear after flowering so it's easy to forget they're there. This will help prevent you planting a new acquisition where you spot an empty space, only to find it's trespassing on another treasure's home. It also helps to know a plant's name when you need to go and look up things like when it needs to be pruned and other care instructions. At the time of planting you may think you'll remember, but three months later you'll be glad you wrote it down.

Right: Labelling new plants will help you remember which plant is where when the growing season gets underway

Types of plants

Once you have everything measured up, know your soil and have made a sketch of your space you can then start to note down a wish list of plants. Keep the style, mood and emotion you'd like to create with your plants in mind at all times. Consider your favourite colours and think about plants in the following groups: trees, shrubs, perennials, bulbs and annuals.

Planting design isn't an exact science, but when choosing plants, try taking these groups one at a time, and looking at their shapes and forms, including leaf shapes and textures. After that consider seasonal interest and, finally, colour and flowers. Once you have a wish list of plants, do a final check to make sure they're right for your soil and the mood you want to create.

TREES

Trees have a trunk and are bigger than shrubs, although you can get multi-stemmed trees. They can also be deciduous or evergreen and there are many varieties suitable for small gardens. Check the spread as this will have more impact in a tight space than the height. Use trees to play with the light and add seasonal interest – think about their ornamental properties, too.

SHRUBS

Shrubs have woody branches and no trunk. They can be deciduous (lose their leaves), semi-evergreen (may keep their leaves in a mild winter) or evergreen (keep their leaves year round). Shrubs offer many attributes including flowers, attractive foliage, adding shape to the border, scent or berries. Shrubs provide structure, an architectural backdrop for your perennial layer, as well as texture and seasonal interest.

5 FOOLPROOF TREES

- *Amelanchier lamarckii*
- Crab apple
- *Euonymus europaeus* 'Red Cascade'
- *Cornus kousa* (right)
- *Acer palmatum* var. dissectum

PERENNIALS

These plants are sometimes referred to as 'herbaceous perennials' and come back year after year. They will usually fill the gaps between your shrubs and can provide a lot of colour through the summer months. They will die back over winter and regrow in the spring.

Hardy geraniums, peonies, penstemons and asters are all good examples of popular perennials. Hardy perennials are left in the ground and although the top growth will disappear over winter, the plant will regrow from its rootstock underground. Some perennials can't cope with cold weather – these are called half-hardy or tender perennials. Check the label to see how low a temperature your plant can tolerate. Some plants such as cannas and tender fuchsias will have to be brought in under cover over winter. Perennials bring contrast, texture, movement, rhythm and seasonal colour.

5 FOOLPROOF SHRUBS

- Japanese skimmia (*Skimmia japonica* subsp. reevesiana)
- Rosa 'Eglantyne'
- Buddleia
- Sweet box (*Sarcococca confusa*) (below)
- Mexican orange blossom (*Choisya ternata*)

5 FOOLPROOF PERENNIALS

- Hardy geraniums
- *Knautia macedonica*
- Pulmonaria 'Blue Ensign'
- Penstemons
- Asters (below)

BULBS

The term 'bulbs' is usually used to describe plants that grow from an underground storage organ. This includes not only true bulbs, but corms, tubers and rhizomes. For example, daffodils grow from true bulbs, but crocus and gladioli grow from corms. Bulbs offer great value and are one of the easiest ways to bring colour to your garden.

ANNUALS

Annuals complete their life cycle in one year. They grow from seed, flower, make more seed and then die. Hardy annuals can withstand cold, so these can be sown outdoors in spring, around March or April. They can also be sown in September. A few examples of hardy annuals include the poppy 'Ladybird', love-in-a-mist and cornflowers. Half-hardy annuals can't survive the cold, so need to be sown indoors in spring. These can then be potted on and planted out once the danger of frost is over – around May or June,

5 FOOLPROOF BULBS

- Tulips
- Dwarf iris
- Daffodils
- Crocus
- Winter aconites (below)

5 FOOLPROOF ANNUALS

- Cosmos
- Sunflowers
- Black-eyed Susan
- Love-in-a-mist
- Nasturtium (below)

depending on where you live. Half-hardy annuals include flowers such as zinnias and cosmos. Annuals are great for experimenting with shape and colour without the commitment of more permanent planting.

BIENNIALS

Biennials live for two years – they are sown in the first year and flower then die in the second year. They are usually sown in late spring or early summer, which gives them time to grow before flowering the following year.

CLIMBERS

These valuable plants are especially useful in a small garden, where they can be used to cover trellis, fences, walls and arches. Even a mix of two or three climbers can provide a huge amount of coverage, adding privacy and colour to your garden. Include an evergreen climber for winter interest. Popular climbers include wisteria, clematis, honeysuckles and jasmine.

---

5 FOOLPROOF BIENNIALS

- Foxgloves (below)
- Sweet rocket
- Sweet William
- Wallflowers
- Honesty

5 FOOLPROOF CLIMBERS

- Common jasmine
- *Clematis cirrhosa*
- Sweet peas (below)
- Spanish flag
- Late-flowering summer clematis

Focus on bulbs

— PROJECT —

HOW TO PLANT BULBS IN A POT

◑ 30 MINUTE TASK
BEST TIME TO DO: OCTOBER–NOVEMBER

You will need:
– Peat-free multi-purpose compost
– 30cm terracotta pot
– Bulbs including daffodil, tulip and crocus

Bulbs are in pots for such a short time that they do not mind being planted shoulder to shoulder. As a rule of thumb ten large-flowered daffodil bulbs can be fitted into a 30cm terracotta pot. You can literally plant them touching each other. The same goes for tulips, although they will still look good if, in the interests of economy, you leave 3–4cm between bulbs. Plant them so that just 5cm of peat-free multi-purpose compost covers the bulbs. They do not need to be planted as deep as bulbs in the garden since in containers they usually form a temporary display. Label them clearly so you can remember those varieties that you especially like.

'Lasagne' planting involves planting layers of bulbs in a pot.

1. Fill your container half-full of peat-free multi-purpose compost and plant a layer of tulips.

2. Add more compost, then plant a layer of daffodils.

3. Add more compost again and plant some crocus bulbs, topping up with compost so that it rests 3cm below the rim of the container to allow for watering. The bulbs will flower in rotation – crocuses first, then daffodils, then tulips. This method gives you, in the words of our friends across the pond, 'more bang for your buck'.

4. After planting, water the bulbs in and stand the containers in a sheltered spot – against a house wall or fence where they are less likely to become waterlogged during the winter. They will need no heat, just shelter from heavy rains. Bring them out on your doorstep, patio or terrace as soon as the shoots begin to emerge in spring so that they have plenty of light and you can watch the shoots grow and the flowers unfurl.

BULB GROWING DOS

○ Choose the right bulbs to suit your growing conditions.

○ Plant bulbs in the ground at three times their own depth and two widths apart.

○ Put them in the ground the right way up. If you can't tell top from bottom, plant them on their side and they'll find their own way.

○ Firm down the compost gently when planting to avoid leaving air gaps around the bulbs.

○ Give the bulbs a good watering in.

○ Protect tulip and crocus bulbs from squirrels by placing chicken wire over them.

BULB GROWING DON'TS

○ Neglect bulbs in pots – they need more watering and feeding than those in the ground.

○ Leave faded blooms in place, as the plant will then waste its energy on producing seed.

○ Cut back foliage until at least six weeks after flowering – wait until it starts to turn yellow.

○ Delay planting – get bulbs in the ground before frost penetrates (tulips can wait until November).

○ Forget where you've planted them – label them so you don't damage them accidentally when weeding or digging after they've died down.

Above left: Bulbs can be planted in the lawn and will come back year after year

Above right: Using a variety of tulip shapes and colours helps to give borders a boost

BULB BUYING TIPS

– Buy each type of bulb as soon as it's available, as the longer bulbs sit around in the shops, the more they dry out. Reject any that feel light and look dehydrated.

– Before you buy, examine the bulbs carefully to ensure they're healthy. Squeeze gently to check they're firm and avoid any with white mould on the surface.

– Look for bigger bulbs, as these produce more flowers. Mail-order firms may use 'top size' to describe the largest bulbs. Others give the circumference. A good size for a tulip is 12cm, *Allium hollandicum* 10–12cm and large narcissi 14–16cm. Hyacinths can be up to 19cm, but about 15cm is ideal and will be more economical to buy.

– Check the flattened base of the bulb to ensure it's healthy and undamaged, as this is where the roots emerge from.

– Some bulbs, particularly daffodils, may have two growing points, or 'noses', which look like two bulbs joined at the base. If both sides are fat, then both are likely to flower. If one side is thin and less developed, it will probably only produce leaves.

Plants for problem spots

Left: *Epimedium* x *warleyense*, ferns and *Tellima grandiflora* thrive in a shady spot

Below left: *Dryopteris affinis* 'Cristata The King'

Below right: *Geranium* 'Rozanne'

DEEP SHADE

This is a situation that most gardeners struggle with. Deep or full shade is usually classed as three hours or less of direct sun each day, and nearly all gardens have some, cast by trees, boundaries or buildings. The first thing to look at is whether the soil is dry or contains moisture. Is there clay or silt, or is it sandy and dry? This is what should influence your plant choices. There are lots of exciting plant combinations to try, especially those with interesting leaf shapes and textures.

Epimediums: These delightful woodland shade-lovers make great ground cover, with heart-shaped leaves and beautiful, delicate flowers in spring. It's best to dig in lots of leafmould when planting.

Dryopteris ferns: Many ferns like shade, but a popular choice is dryopteris. The fronds bring beautiful texture, and many species hold their leaves right through the winter.

Hardy geraniums: These are such versatile plants – different species like different positions, but many thrive in full shade, flowering profusely. After the first flush of early blooms, cut them back hard and they'll soon come back with strong lush growth and often a second flush of flowers.

PARTIAL SHADE

This could be an area that's shaded for only part of the day, or gets mainly dappled light from the canopy of a tree or large shrub. Understanding the soil is important – is it free-draining or does it hold moisture? Unlike other situations, plants labelled 'full sun' will usually grow quite happily in partial shade, although they might flower less prolifically. It's worth experimenting.

Astrantias: These perennials are wonderful plants for shade, and they keep producing their beautiful pincushion flowers, right through the summer months. Many species are happy in semi-shade, although some need more sun, while others prefer more shade.

Grasses: Ornamental grasses are a wonderful addition to a planting scheme and calamagrostis is one of the best, bringing structure to any border. They bring movement to a garden in even the softest breeze, and also provide interest right through the winter months.

Viburnums: These hard-working shrubs provide flowers, berries, bold structure and foliage that is often evergreen or may have colourful tints. Many varieties grow happily in semi-shade, with some even providing valuable winter flowers and scent.

From left to right: Astrantia, *Calamagrostis x acutiflora* 'Karl Foerster', *Buddleia davidii* 'Orpheus', *Kniphofia* 'Limelight'

FULL SUN

This is something that every gardener seems to crave, and a south-facing garden is considered a big asset. However, if you have a sun trap, then your soil will dry out very easily, especially during summer. While this is the perfect opportunity to create a Mediterranean paradise, or a gravel garden full of drought-tolerant plants, other plants will find the conditions very tough.

Buddleias: These shrubs will grow in so many situations, but they especially enjoy a sunny site. Different varieties offer flowers in a range of colours, from white to pink to deep purple. They flower throughout the summer and are a magnet for butterflies. There are dwarf varieties too, if you're short on space.

Red-hot pokers: These are perfect for a sunny spot, adding vertical drama from June to September. Also known as kniphofias, they come in a wide choice of colours, from fiery orange to lemon yellow, and even pale green.

Phlomis: These evergreen perennials love sunny, well-drained conditions. Try them not only for their hooded flowers, but for the seedheads that provide structure throughout winter.

EXPOSED AND WINDY

Think of an exposed site, and coastal gardens come to mind. But inland gardens can be windy too, depending on their location and aspect, and whether there are buildings and boundaries nearby – either protecting them or creating turbulence. It can be difficult to establish plants on a windy site, so when you're planting you may need to provide temporary shelter. It makes sense to look at other local gardens or the wider landscape for planting inspiration.

Eryngiums: These bring great texture and shape to a planting scheme. Also known as sea holly, they are easy and really accommodating plants, in colours from electric blue to frosty white. They can be used with great success in well-drained soil on exposed sites.

Tamarisk: This shrub or small tree has feathery foliage and pink flowers in late summer. It's really useful on exposed sites and makes a good windbreak.

Centranthus: A familiar sight in many British coastal resorts throughout the summer, this perennial comes in red, pink or white forms. It's happy in poor, well-drained soil and self-seeds freely.

From left to right: *Eryngium planum, Centranthus ruber, Trollius* 'Dancing Flame'

DAMP OR SATURATED SOIL

Waterlogged soil can be tough to cope with in winter, but in summer it has great potential to come alive with colour, just when other areas are becoming more difficult. Many plants hate having their roots in water, so instead of making them struggle, embrace your wet soil and create a bog garden full of vibrant plants that love these conditions. If you really want to grow plants that prefer a less soggy site, you'll need to improve the drainage by digging in lots of organic matter or installing drains.

Trollius: Globeflowers are buttercup relatives and love damp soil. There are lots of varieties, with flower colours ranging from strong orange to soft yellow. They work really well in a bog garden.

Siberian irises: Tall and elegant, these irises love soil that doesn't dry out. The early summer flowers range from white to yellow to blue and velvety purple, while the foliage provides a great upright to plant against.

Rodgersias: These are fantastic for bog gardens. They have big textured leaves that are really dramatic and they send up tall fluffy spires of pink or white flowers in summer, too.

DRY OR LIGHT SOIL

Soil that is either sandy or very stony tends to drain really quickly. It's easy to dig and warms up quickly in spring, but nutrients are easily washed out, as is any moisture. Dry shade is probably the most difficult to work with, so dig in plenty of organic matter every year and keep the planting simple. Try a few different plants, and find two or three that work well and then repeat them.

Right: Artemisia 'Powis Castle' grows well in light soil

Sedums: These succulent plants grow happily in a sandy, sunny position. There are lots of varieties, of various sizes and colours, that will flower for most of the summer. Great for gravel gardens.

Thymes: This culinary herb comes in several different colours of foliage and flowers, as well as different scents. The low-growing plants work really well as ground cover in gravel and you can use them en masse to great effect.

Artemisias: Like many grey-leaved plants, artemisias love full sun and light soil. Their lovely silver-tinged foliage works well with so many other plants.

TOP TIP

Add height with see-through plants
Traditional border design sees plants layered up in tiers like theatre seats, but you can make a border more dynamic by adding tall see-through plants. Light, elegant species such as some ornamental grasses, *Verbena bonariensis* and *Salvia uliginosa*, work perfectly in this situation. Their leggy form and small footprint mean they can be slotted in between shorter plants in the middle of the border, without taking up much ground space. They add height without bulk, create a punctuation in the planting and allow you to see surrounding colour and form through them. This then generates extra colour combinations and contrasts.

Choose a style

Cottage: This is the look to go for if you like a jumble of flowers and foliage, especially around an old house. A mixture of colours is usual, but go steady on the ornamental grasses. Roses fit in well. Keep it simple by limiting the amount of plants you use. Good climbers to use include clematis and honeysuckle.

Prairie: Grasses are important, interwoven with perennials such as rudbeckias, echinaceas, kniphofias and the like. You'll soon get a feel for it. Bulbs like camassias and galtonias work well to extend the season.

Herbaceous: The traditional herbaceous border works best on a large scale. Be sweeping with your drifts, rather than dotting plants about. Many of them will need some kind of support, and a trickle irrigation system will be a real boon.

Above: A mix of hydrangeas and climbing roses are well suited to a cottage garden look

Above right: *Miscanthus sinensis* adds a prairie style look to a border of asters and helianthus

Right: Large-leaved foliage plants such as bananas create an exotic look

Contemporary: Suited to modern houses and usually uses a limited selection of plants and hard landscaping that ties in with the house. Go for spectacular planting in simple swirls and drifts, with dramatic architectural specimens, as well as lumps of rock, sheets of water and seas of gravel.

Tropical: Massive foliage of bananas, cannas and ginger lilies, plus brilliant flowers of dahlias, impatiens and other bedders make a tropical scheme one of the most vibrant, but its season of interest may be quite short, from June to October.

How to combine plants

Left: Red canna flowers dotted through the border provide height and colour

Overleaf: A jumble of dahlias, snapdragons and sunflowers add colour to deep borders

Star quality: You need several points of interest, such as large leaved cannas. Set these off with 'fillers' and 'carpeters', arranged to create an undulating display where each plant, particularly the stars, stands out as an individual instead of vanishing into the mêlée.

Vary the heights: Create groups of plants in threes to make roughly triangular shapes – one taller/upright, one domed and one low/spreading. Make use of contrasts, especially in textures (foliage can be furry, shiny or matte) and shapes – of leaves, flowers or whole plants.

Picture perfect: Creating a border is, in many ways, like painting a picture – a landscape, naturally. You need to think about your background (a hedge, fence, or taller plants), your foreground (dwarf edging, low-creeping perennials such as certain geranium species, or short annuals), and your middle distance (the bulk of your display) to give the scene depth.

Be bold: Smallish borders can be designed around one large centrepiece plant – *Crambe cordifolia* for instance – but as long as you choose one with a long 'peak' season or a series of changing attractions, the effect can be brilliant. It's especially eye-catching because few people dare to break the mould in this way. You can use small plants in borders, but instead of dotting one here and there, the trick is to be bold and plant groups of three or five so that they make their mark.

5 EASY BORDER SUPPORT ACTS
Backdrop plants are key to successful combinations.

Lady's mantle: *Alchemilla mollis* is low, leafy and easy-going, with foamy lime-green flowers – brilliant for pulling a busy border together.

Verbena bonariensis: Tall plants creating a misty, light-purple haze in the top tier of a scheme based on shrubs, roses or taller perennials.

Buxus sempervirens (box): Use as dwarf edging or in clipped balls to help create a nice hint of 'formal' along the front of a flower border.

Hardy geraniums: With a great colour spectrum, they provide brilliant ground cover for the basement of mixed borders.

Ornamental grasses: These are the foundation of contemporary 'designer' schemes and prairie-style plantings, adding texture and movement.

Keep it cool

At its peak: May
Pale blue flowers are great
for shady corners as they
bounce light around, and
this delicate little bellflower
shines out against the lush
green ferns.

The plants

1. *Dryopteris filix-mas*
   H x S 100cm x 100cm
   Care: Likes cool shade
   and humus-rich soil

2. *Campanula* 'Samantha'
   H x S 25cm x 30cm
   Care: Free draining soil
   in sun or shade

Opposites attract

At its peak: June
This dramatic pairing contrasts both form and colour. Horizontal daisies of pale ivory astrantia make the perfect foil to the soaring spires of blue salvia.

The plants

1. *Salvia nemorosa* 'Caradonna'
   H x S 50cm x 30cm
   Care: Deadhead flowers as they fade

2. *Astrantia* 'Shaggy'
   H x S 80cm x 35cm
   Care: Enjoys moist but free-draining soil

Annuals with attitude

At its peak: July
Bold combinations of easy-care annuals in electric hot colours like these magenta pink cosmos and vibrant orange marigolds will turn heads.

The plants

1. *Cosmos bipinnatus* 'Dazzler'
   H x S 100cm x 60cm
   Care: Sow direct April–May

2. *Calendula officinalis*
   H x S 50cm x 30cm
   Care: Deadhead to prolong flowering

Bold statement

At its peak: June–August
A glorious clash of scarlet, jubilant pink and violet blue will lift and draw the eye to any sunny border in the summer. The mounding green foliage of the old-fashioned coral bells (heuchera) forms a neat contrast to the riot of colour above. Deadhead the heuchera and cut out the salvia flower spikes as soon as they begin to fade, leaving the foliage to take on russet tones in the autumn.

The plants

1. *Phlox paniculata* 'Franz Schubert'
   H x S: 90cm x 30cm
   Care: Support plant before flowering to prevent flopping

2. *Salvia pratensis*
   H x S: 1m x 50cm
   Care: Cut the flower spikes when they begin to fade

3. Heuchera with green foliage such as *Heuchera* 'Firefly'
   H x S: 50cm x 45cm
   Care: Deadhead the heuchera after flowering

Three Degrees

At its peak: June–July

Spikes of indigo purple and flashes of hot orange are woven through a blue-grey sea. With wispy flowerheads in early summer, the neat mounds of the blue helictotrichon harmonise brilliantly with the elegant salvia spikes and the sunset-orange poppies.

The plants

1. *Salvia pratensis*
   H x S: 1m x 50cm
   Care: Cut the flower spikes when they begin to fade

2. *Helictotrichon sempervirens*
   H x S: 1.4m x 1m
   Care: Comb through the grass to remove dead leaves and spent flower spikes

3. *Papaver nudicaule*
   H x S: 45cm x 25cm
   Care: Sow the poppies in autumn and allow to self-seed freely each year.

CHOOSING PLANTS DOS

○ Earmark a location before you buy a plant (well, try to do it that way round).

○ Check the ultimate spread of a tree before you buy it – it's more important than the height.

○ Plant daffodils in clumps – space 10 or 12 bulbs 4cm apart, rather than planting in wide-spaced drifts, for best effect.

○ Buy from local nurseries, both to give them support and because plants grown locally will usually do best in your garden.

○ Get the most from your border by including evergreen plants for year-round interest, and then adding bulbs and long-flowering annuals and perennials for bursts of seasonal interest.

CHOOSING PLANTS DON'TS

○ Don't include dominant plants. In a small border, take care to avoid 'thugs' that will spread rampantly and swamp everything else. Mint, Japanese anemones, bear's breeches (acanthus) and the spreading reed canary grass (*Phalaris arundinacea*) can all take over a border.

○ Don't force a plant into a spot it won't thrive in. Before you buy a plant be sure it will suit the light levels and soil. Read plant labels and do your research.

○ Don't plant in a scattergun way. Avoid a messy border by repeating plants through the scheme to bind it together. Buy several of the same plant, or large pots of perennials that you can divide.

Jargon buster

Left: Dahlias, rudbeckias and cannas add colour to a vibrant border

Below: Red salvias and purple lupins make a striking colour combination

Herbaceous – this means the plant isn't woody; it has soft stems.

Under cover – indoors under glass, e.g. a greenhouse or conservatory.

Deciduous – leaves fall in autumn.

Evergreen – leaves stay year round.

Actions:
– Decide on a planting style
– Choose the plants for your garden

CHAPTER FOUR

Right plant, right time

Right plant, right time

Left: Water young plants regularly until they are established

There is nothing more wonderful when you're creating a garden than getting your hands on new plants or growing your own from seed. It's a big opportunity to bring the space to life with a selection of plants that will provide structure, colour, form and texture to your displays. Design is important, but it's the plants that attract wildlife and connect us to our gardens through every one of our senses.

That said, many people get anxious when it comes to sowing seed and planting up a border, and worry that they are going to kill things. But it's easy to get these techniques right when you follow a few basic rules. When sowing, start with something simple that will germinate quickly. Try California poppies, nasturtiums, sweet peas or cosmos – these are all easy to grow and one packet of seed will provide you with plenty of flowers to transform pots or borders.

When planting, it's all about preparing the soil well and taking the time to give plants the conditions they need. Most plants are best planted out in autumn or spring, when the soil is warm and moist, but you can plant container-grown plants year round. Just avoid periods of extreme heat or cold, when the ground will be dry or frozen. Check each individual plant's requirements and it's easy to provide our plants with the best possible start in our plots.

Core skills:
– Sowing seed
– Planting perennials
– Planting trees and shrubs
– Pricking out seedlings

5 steps to success

1. **Get the timing right.** It always pays to be prompt when gardening. Doing things at the right time is hugely important and can mean the difference between success and failure. Timing is everything. Simple practices like getting plants in the ground as soon as you've found the right place for them, rather than leaving them beside the path and 'coming back to them', will save you wasting time trying to resuscitate them and save the expense of having to buy more plants.

2. **Prepare planting areas.** All new plants will be happier if it's easy for their roots to move outwards away from the plant. This will help secure them in the ground and take up water and nutrients. To give them the best start, make sure the soil is in 'good heart' – by which we mean it's healthy and fertile. Once your borders or planting areas are marked out, start preparing your soil by digging over the beds with a fork or spade, clearing any large stones and old roots and breaking up large clods as you turn the ground. Clear any weeds – you don't want your new plants having to compete for water, food and light. Next, dig in organic matter, such as compost or well-rotted manure. If possible do this a month or two before you start planting. If you can't do that, get the organic matter in a week or two before planting. If drainage is an issue, it's a good idea to add some grit to your soil before planting. If the ground is really dry, you can add more organic matter to help the soil retain moisture.

3. **Look after new plants.** Always make sure plants have adequate water. Letting them dry out for even a couple of days can hinder their progress. Water thoroughly, drenching the soil around the plant. When soil is moist apply a thick mulch of spent mushroom compost, leafmould, or best of all, garden compost. The thicker the better. This will help conserve moisture and keep weeds to a minimum. Once you're certain that plants are getting established, evidenced by new shoots and fresh growth, feed them regularly with a very dilute organic liquid feed such as seaweed extract. Always apply feed when the soil is moist.

4. **Judge timing based on location.** Anything planted in autumn needs to be robust enough to get its roots into the surrounding soil and for them to continue to make headway over the winter. If your soil is heavy and prone to waterlogging, it is wise to wait until spring to plant anything that hates winter wet – achilleas are a prime example. It is also wise to avoid autumn planting for any plants, be they herbaceous shrubs or perennials, whose hardiness is at all questionable. And as with any advice, local conditions need to be taken into account. A lavender or *Convolvulus cneorum*, which would be perfectly happy planted out in October in a warm border in free-draining soil on the south coast,

Above: Tip the plant gently out of its pot before planting and tease out its roots

would turn up its toes lowered into cold, wet soil in North Yorkshire. Use common sense, knowledge of your own location, soil and level of exposure.

(5) Use the right compost. Seed-sowing compost should be free draining and doesn't need to have lots of nutrients; in fact, rich composts can stunt the growth of young plants. Instead of buying a special seed compost, you can use standard multi-purpose compost and add around 50 per cent of coarse sand, grit, vermiculite or perlite to increase aeration around your seeds and seedlings. Unfortunately, composts vary in quality, so it's worth doing a bit of research to find the one that suits you best.

Planting potted perennials

First arrange the plants in the bed while they're still in their pots – with the help of a planting plan if you're using one, or by eye. Check the labels to see how big each will grow, so you know how much space to leave between them.

Now it's time to start planting. Plant one at a time. Make sure you're generous with the size of the hole – a good guide is to dig a hole twice the width of the pot or rootball. Knock your plant from its pot and tease out the roots to stimulate growth.

Position the plant in the hole so the top of the compost is no deeper than the soil surface. Back-fill with soil, firm it gently, then water in well.

Below: Position plants in their pots to see how they look

Planting trees and shrubs

Above left: The planting hole should be the same depth as the plant's rootball

Above right: Fill in around your tree or shrub and firm it in

Deciduous trees and shrubs are available either in containers (plastic or fabric) or with bare roots (while they are dormant). Evergreens, however, are only sold in containers, as they don't go into full dormancy.

Trees and shrubs in containers can be planted at any time of year, though ideally not in hot weather. Bare-root plants are only available from November to late March, for immediate planting. Before buying, make sure you have enough space for the plant's eventual height and spread.

It is important to dig a planting hole that is the right shape and depth. A common mistake is planting too deeply, in a hole that's not wide enough. Dig a square hole – if you dig a small, round hole, it's like creating a slightly larger pot, and the roots will grow in a circular way, rather than outwards to anchor the plant.

If you have poor soil, sprinkle mycorrhizal fungi onto the roots before planting. These beneficial fungi should help the roots to function more effectively.

Water well after planting to settle the soil. Keep on watering regularly for the first couple of years, especially in summer. New trees also need staking.

IN A CONTAINER

Dig a square hole, twice the width of the rootball. Check the size of the rootball against your hole to ensure it's the right depth. Soak the plant before planting. Back-fill the soil, firming with your foot. Make sure the soil is fine, so it has contact with the roots and there aren't any air pockets. Then stand back to check the trunk is vertical.

BARE ROOT

Dig a hole twice the width of the root system. Before planting, cut off any damaged roots. The secret of success when you are planting any bare-root specimen is to avoid dehydration. Before you plant, always soak their roots in a bucket of water overnight and after planting make sure the soil does not dry out. A liberal helping of organic matter – well-rotted garden compost or manure added to the soil – will help moisture retention.

Plant roses so that the graft union (where the stems meet the rootstock) is a couple of inches below the level of the soil. This will make for greater stability. Where trees more than a metre high are concerned, give them a stake – knocked in at an angle of 45° – and a tree tie to keep them upright in strong winds. On all but the tallest trees it's a good idea to choose trees that are no taller than yourself, as they establish more readily than larger specimens. You should be able to remove the stake after a year's growth, since the roots will offer sufficient anchorage.

Why buy bare root? Bare-root plants are sold between November and March. They arrive looking like twigs, with no soil, but this is a much cheaper way to buy trees and shrubs and if you plant them out in autumn, while the soil is still moist and warm from summer, you have great conditions for the tree to establish. There is far less likelihood of drying out than in summer when planting out a container-grown tree.

**Above left: Roses
are cheaper to buy
as bare-root plants**

**Above right: Hostas thrive
in moist, shady spots**

TOP BARE-ROOT PLANTS TO BUY

– **Roses:** Perhaps the most resilient of all shrubs, roses have a great capacity to survive upheaval and cost so much less than those sold in containers.

– **Fruit trees:** Especially those which are younger and ready to be trained. Larger, trained specimens are best planted out from containers.

– **Soft fruits:** Currants, gooseberries and raspberries will establish well and cost just a fraction of those sold growing individually in containers. Bare-root strawberries, too, will grow away happily.

– **Hedging plants:** By far the most economical way of buying a hedge – especially if you have a long run to plant.

– **Hostas:** The fat roots of hostas are resistant to drying out and will enjoy the moisture of autumn.

HOW TO SUPPORT NEW PLANTS

◑ 30 MINUTE TASK
BEST TIME TO DO: NOVEMBER–MAY

You will need:
– Wooden tree stake
  (diameter 75mm)
– Handsaw
– Lump hammer
– Rubber ties
– Nails
– Support canes

Most new trees need staking, otherwise they'll be blown around by the wind, and this movement loosens the roots and hinders establishment. The stake should hold the lower part of the trunk stable and let the upper part flex, so it is best positioned at a 45° angle, on the side that receives the prevailing wind. For a containerised tree, hammer the stake into the ground after planting, avoiding the rootball. Secure the tree to the stake with a rubber tie, then saw off the excess stake with care. With bare-root trees, you can hammer in the stake before you back-fill around the plant with soil.

Some tall perennials, such as delphiniums, will need supporting with canes to stop them flopping over, and it's best to do this before they get too established. Just push the canes into the soil, taking care not to damage the roots, then tie the stems to them as they grow over the season. Avoid tying the stems too tightly.

When to sow seeds

Timing is everything when it comes to seed sowing – do it too early and seeds may not germinate; leave it too late and plants may not have enough time to grow. And the right time to sow changes from year to year and place to place. So how can you ensure you get it right every time?

For some plants there's a wide window of time in which you can successfully sow seeds, for others it's more precise. But whether you're after flowers or veg, sowing at the right time for that plant will give you more reliable germination and bigger, healthier plants, with more crops to harvest or flowers to enjoy. You can also avoid many common pests and problems by getting your timing right.

HEAT THINGS UP

Seeds require warmth to germinate and some seedlings need even more warmth to thrive. Sow too early, when the soil and air are still cold and damp, and you'll get rotting seeds and low germination rates, or seedlings that fail to thrive.

Tender plants, such as French beans and zinnias, demand higher temperatures than hardy plants such as onions and poppies, so check the plant's needs before you sow. You can protect seeds by sowing under cover or covering outdoor sowings with a fleece or cloche, but it's better to wait for warmer weather, and use protection to guard against sudden temperature drops.

WAIT FOR THE LIGHT

Once seeds have germinated, the seedlings will need as much daylight as possible. There are around two hours more daylight on 31 March compared with 1 March, and the difference in day length is more pronounced the further north you are, so it's even more beneficial to delay your sowings.

If you're sowing under cover, ensuring greenhouse glass is clean and moving seedlings to a spot where they'll receive light from at least three sides will help them soak up what brightness there is.

FEAR THE FROST

Look up dates for last frosts in your area and keep a keen eye on the weather forecasts. You'll need to wait until April or later before sowing tender plants outdoors in spring, but also ensure you are on time with summer sowings of plants susceptible to early autumn frosts. If spring is extra cold or you live in a place with a short growing season, it pays to sow plants that need a long growing season closer to the right time under cover, rather than waiting until late in the year and risking autumn frosts.

AVOID PESTS AND DISEASES

Many common pests and diseases can be sidestepped by timing your sowing carefully. For example, sowing salad rocket in early August will mean you avoid flea beetle, and sowing peas early in the year helps them to crop before pea moths arrive in July. Plants that have been sown direct early in the year, when the weather is cool, will be growing slowly and will be vulnerable to slugs – either sow later in the year, sow under cover and plant out when warmer, or use plenty of slug defences.

EXCEPTIONS TO THE RULES

While most plants concentrate on growing roots and leaves in spring, some also flower, which is fine if you want flowers, but once an annual or biennial plant has flowered it stops making new leaves. Veg in this category are best sown after the June solstice to avoid bolting. Wait until July to sow Florence fennel and radicchio, and early August to sow endive, salad rocket, oriental leaves, chervil, land cress and claytonia. Sow Sweet William and wallflowers in summer, too.

Below: Coldframes provide protection for tender and young plants

WHEN TO SOW UNDER COVER

Starting under cover increases your growing season by up to a month, so is especially useful in colder areas, during cool, damp springs and for plants that need a long growing season. Plants that are happy in cool conditions – such as spinach, cabbage, lettuce, cornflowers and sweet peas – can be sown under cover as early as February. But frost-susceptible plants must be sown later to be the right size to plant out after your last spring frost date. Remember, while you can add warmth by sowing under cover, you can't make the days longer.

WHEN TO SOW OUTDOORS

Most seeds need a soil temperature of at least 6°C, preferably higher – usually after mid-March in southern Britain and early April in the north, but it varies depending on the year and soil type. Use a soil thermometer or stick a finger deep into the soil. If it's uncomfortably cold, then it's too early to sow. If your seeds are cheap and you have lots, you could just try a batch and see what happens. But if you're unsure, wait a week and reassess – seeds sown later in warmer, brighter weather will usually catch up with, and even overtake, those sown too early.

TOP TIP

Weather varies from year to year, but your location and soil are constant, and sowing dates should be adapted to suit your conditions. There are general guidelines to follow – the best sowing dates for northern Britain are one to three weeks later than in the south. Sow later if you are at high altitude, exposed to wind or in a frost pocket. Sow earlier in sandy soil and later in heavy clay as it will take longer to warm up.

Make your knowledge more specific by keeping a gardening diary. It will help you build up a more accurate picture of your conditions, and you'll see patterns emerging as you refer back from year to year. Here are some of the things to record in your diary, but add others that strike you through the year:

- **Dates** of sowing, planting, flowering and harvesting

- **Germination** success rates

- **The varieties** you sowed

- **Cropping** or flowering results

- **Problems** with pests and diseases, or weak growth

- **Weather** – you don't need to be as specific as exact temperatures and rainfall measurements, just note generally whether the month was warm, dull, wet or windy

HOW TO SOW INDOORS

15 MINUTE TASK
BEST TIME TO DO: JANUARY–APRIL

You will need:
– Seed compost
– Small pots or a seed tray
– Sieve
– Seeds
– Watering can

1. Fill the pot or tray loosely to the brim with peat-free seed compost. Tap it to settle the compost, then lightly tamp it level with a wooden firmer or the base of a flowerpot. The surface of the compost should be about a centimetre below the rim of the container.

2. Sow the seeds thinly so they sit about a centimetre apart. Larger seeds, such as sweet peas, can be spaced out individually.

3. Cover the seeds with compost – there are just a few exceptions: fine seeds such as begonias and petunias need no covering at all. Most seeds, though, should be covered with a layer of compost equal to their diameter.

Use a sieve (or plastic flowerpot), shaking it from side to side over the sown seeds until they disappear. That's usually all they need. Larger seeds can be covered with slightly more compost – about twice their diameter.

4. Water to dampen the compost. For larger seeds you can use a watering can fitted with a fine rose (sprinkler head), but be gentle as there's a risk of washing the seeds out of place. Finer seeds are particularly easy to dislodge, so instead stand the container in a tray or saucer of water for an hour and let the compost absorb what it needs. Label the container. To make conditions even more favourable for germination, put the tray or pot in a heated propagator. Windowsill versions are available and are well worth the modest investment.

HOW TO SOW OUTDOORS

15 MINUTE TASK
BEST TIME TO DO: APRIL–JUNE, DEPENDING ON SEED

You will need:
– Garden fork
– Hand trowel
– Seeds
– Watering can

1. Fork over the area and use a rake or hand trowel to get rid of lumps in the soil until you have a fine, crumbly texture. Make a drill using a hoe or trowel handle.

2. Sow the seeds along the prepared trench at the distance stated on the seed packet.

3. Draw soil back over the seeds so they are at the correct depth. Water in well using a watering can fitted with a fine rose.

How to sow successfully

There's nothing more frustrating than seeds that don't germinate or seedlings that keel over. But by making sure you sow your seeds under the best possible conditions, you can give them the best chance of success.

It's worth getting your sowing really spot on, not just for the money it will save you compared with buying plants, but also because homegrown plants are often stronger than bought ones, which have been carefully cosseted in industrial polytunnels. Little details like where you sow, the compost and container you use, and how deep you sow all add up to affect your seeds' performance. Grow good sowing habits and you'll relish the results.

Sowing seeds under cover will help improve your germination rates through the extra warmth and protection from pests. Even seeds you think need to be sown direct, such as coriander and hardy annuals, can be raised under cover and planted out – which is beneficial if you have heavy soil or are in a cold spot.

Direct sowing is best limited to fast growers, large seeds, plants that tolerate cool conditions, and tap-root veg such as carrots and parsnips. Most seeds have a 'temperature threshold' below which their seeds lie dormant. If you are sowing in late winter to early spring, or you're sowing tender plants, such as basil, chillies and zinnias, you'll get better germination if you add warmth from a propagator or by placing sown seeds on a windowsill over a radiator.

WATER CAREFULLY

Water compost thoroughly before sowing seeds. After this, water only when you see signs of the compost drying around its edges, until the plants are really growing. This helps avoid damping off – when small seedlings fall over and rot. If your seedlings still succumb, try sowing more thinly, so that air can pass between the stems.

GET THE DEPTH RIGHT

Few seeds profit from being buried too deep – they are better at sending roots down than pushing up new stems through lots of compost or soil. Cover seeds with enough compost or vermiculite to just hide them. Push larger seeds into modules or pots so they are just below the surface. At most, seeds should be covered with twice their own width in compost. Seeds such as antirrhinum, primula and celery need light to germinate, and so should be sown on the surface of the compost.

Right: Labelling pots of seeds will help you identify seedlings

WHAT TO SOW IN

Tiny seeds that germinate slowly are best sown in seed trays, so that you can prick out the strongest. Do this when seedlings have the first two leaves. Use a pencil to prise up the roots of a clump and pull out one seedling at a time, holding its leaves. Make a deep hole in the compost in a module tray and drop or coil the root into the hole with the stems buried to encourage sturdy growth. Medium-sized seeds, such as beetroot, are best sown in modules, and large seeds, such as sunflowers, in 9–10cm pots.

AFTER CARE

When seedlings first emerge, they're at their most vulnerable. Make sure they're in bright (but not scorching) light and never allow the compost to dry out. If light levels are poor, the seedlings will become spindly, while overly bright sun may scorch their delicate leaves.

As soon as they're large enough to handle, ease them from their comfortable bed of compost and into a new container to give them more room to grow. This is known as 'pricking out'. Bedding plants are usually transferred to seed trays and spaced 5cm apart. Plants to be grown in containers can be pricked out singly into 8cm pots. In all cases, use fresh peat-free multi-purpose compost.

Below: When seedlings are big enough and have their first set of true leaves, it's time to prick them out

PRICKING OUT

Never handle seedlings by their stems. Hold one of the first 'seed leaves' (cotyledons) carefully between your finger and thumb and lever out the roots using the pointed end of a pencil. Lift the seedling out, make a hole in the compost in the new tray and lower the roots in. Gently firm the compost with the pencil so the seedling sits at the same level it was previously growing. If the seedlings are a little long in the stem, there is usually no reason why they cannot be buried a little deeper to give them more stability.

Really small seeds such as those of begonias produce tiny plants that need to be carefully eased out of their seed tray with the pointed end of a pencil and simply 'shuffled' into the surface of the new tray of compost. These tiny seedlings are best watered from below (as with the seeds), but most others can be watered from above using a watering can with a fine rose.

Cover pricked-out seedlings with a single sheet of newspaper for the first day or two until they're standing upright, then give them as much light as possible.

HARDENING OFF SEEDLINGS

Bedding plants can stay in their trays until it's time to plant them out. Plants to be grown in containers should be 'potted on' (moved to a larger container) when they outgrow their first home. Pinch out the shoot tips as the plants grow to encourage them to bush out.

If the plants are destined for the garden, they should be 'hardened off' by gradually introducing them to lower temperatures and the great outdoors. Do this in stages, giving them more and more ventilation until they're outdoors by day but brought in at night.

Once fully acclimatised and, in the case of tender bedding, the danger of frost is past (usually late May or early June), they can be planted out with impunity and you can give yourself a pat on the back.

SOWING AND PLANTING DOS

○ Sow fresh seeds. Seeds lose their viability with age – sometimes after only a year.

○ Prepare your planting area – preparation is key whenever you're planting, but especially when planting in the autumn. You need to maximise the chances of plants getting established so add plenty of organic matter to the planting mix and surrounding soil.

○ Break the roots of pot-bound plants using a hand fork vertically all around the root ball. This will encourage the formation of fine, feeding roots and help your plant move out into the surrounding soil.

○ Keep new plants well watered – fill planting holes with water and allow it to drain away before planting. Soak plants thoroughly before planting and water in well afterwards. Watering is vital to get plants off to a good start, even when soil is moist.

○ Add grit to the bottom of the planting hole to help drainage, if your soil is particularly heavy.

○ Protect newly planted subjects with newspaper or bubble wrap in the event of an unseasonal frost.

○ Cut back foliage, especially of evergreens growing in open ground, such as pulmonarias and brunnera. This will encourage them to make roots as there will be less demand to keep excess foliage going.

SOWING AND PLANTING DON'TS

○ Don't leave seedlings too long before pricking out. Overcrowded seedlings are more likely to suffer from diseases and they may grow spindly as they reach for the light .

○ Don't sow too early – seeds sown too early may suffer due to low temperatures (if not given enough heat) and fail to thrive. Seed packets give recommended temperatures for sowing and growing on.

○ Don't sow too deeply – if seedlings fail to appear, the seeds may have been sown too deeply or may require light to germinate. Never sow more deeply than twice the diameter of the seed.

○ Avoid planting into a sump! Break up the soil in the bottom of a planting hole to help water drain away. While you're at it, fork over soil over a wide radius around the planting hole to prevent compaction.

○ Let weeds take over – weeds compete for resources (both water and nutrients) so keep on top of it, especially around new plants.

Above right: Keep newly planted seedlings well watered

Jargon buster

Damping off – the term used for fungal ailments, usually affecting seedlings by causing the stem to rot off at soil level

Drill – narrow furrow in the soil for sowing seed

Hardening off – the process of acclimatising plants to lower temperatures, usually following their raising under cover, before planting outside (below left)

Pricking out – transplanting seedlings from the seed beds in which they were sown to new, larger receptacles (below right)

Actions:
- Feel soil to see if it's warm enough to sow
- Keep a record of what and where you've sown seeds
- Label any trees, perennials or shrubs that you plant so it's easy to look up aftercare requirements later

CHAPTER FIVE

Use your space wisely

Use your space wisely

Left: Shelving adds more planting opportunities and brings colour to a bare wall

If you have a tiny garden or patio, there are several ways to make more of your space. No room for a border? Plant up a container or two and change the look seasonally. You could add colour to windowsills and entrances with hanging baskets and window boxes. Or plant a permanent pot – choose a shrub or tree for a pot as your main plant, which will look good all year – then simply add in seasonal underplanting, from winter flowering pansies to summer bedding, to change the look.

Vertical gardening provides an opportunity to fill your garden with plants if you are short on ground space. Even a short stretch of fence will have room for two or three climbers if you choose the right types. Combine an evergreen climber for winter interest with spring and summer flowering climbers so there's always something attractive to look at. Not only will this add a colour boost to your garden, but it will provide privacy from neighbours, too.

Core skills:
– Planting a container
– Choosing plants for a boundary

5 steps to success

1. **Take care when positioning your containers.** Most plants like good light, but if your spot is shady, then choose plants that thrive in low light levels – ferns, hostas, ivy and numerous other shade-lovers. Sites exposed to wind will exacerbate drying out, not only of the compost but of delicate leaves on plants such as Japanese maples. A windbreak is a good idea on exposed balconies – you can use close-weave netting or willow hurdles strapped to the balustrading.

2. **Choose plants that offer a long season of interest** – for boundaries classic climbers such as clematis and roses thrive on walls and provide up to six months of flowers.

3. **Use a tiered stand** if you want lots of containers but have little ground space. This makes an eye-catching feature, too. If you think of your garden as a box with just two planes, one horizontal and one vertical, available room soon runs out in a small space. Staging is a great way to increase your growing area.

4. **Make more of your windowsills.** These tiny spaces can bring a single window or a whole building to life. Bedding plants such as pansies and petunias are the mainstay of most window boxes – these flowers have been bred to flower for months. Other things you could try include miniature spring bulbs, heather and ivy or edibles such as tumbling tomatoes and chillies.

5. **Choose a boundary solution that you have time to maintain.** Hedges are high input, while walls are low fuss. If you need low maintenance, choose climbers that you don't need to prune, such as winter or spring-flowering clematis, or light pruning such as star jasmine (*Trachelospermum jasminoides*). Star jasmine will also add fragrance to the garden.

Right: Ajuga, ferns and bleeding heart make attractive plant partners for a container in the shade

Container gardening

Left: Terracotta pots are an attractive option for a vibrant dahlia display

Nowhere do gardeners wield more power than when we grow plants in containers. The basic ingredients of plant growth are food, water, light and air, and in containers we – rather than Mother Nature – are responsible for supplying at least the first three of these things. As long as we do that, container gardening offers us tremendous versatility – a chance to grow plants where there's no earth for them to root into, no space for huge displays or where the growing conditions would otherwise be inhospitable to their wellbeing.

Another major benefit of containers is that they can be moved around at will, giving you the ability to change your outlook as often as you wish. In short, container gardening is the best way of refreshing a garden without the need for any huge upheavals, provided you remember that the secret of success is generosity with food and water.

WHAT TYPE OF CONTAINER?

When choosing a container, look for one that will hold enough compost to sustain your plants and allows water to drain out. If you grow plants in containers without drainage holes, there is a risk they'll literally drown – especially in damp British winters.

Choose as large a container as you have room for. Big containers give plants more compost to root into, and they'll be better fed and watered as a result, so their growth will be much healthier. Added to which, from a design point of view, three or four sizeable containers always look more striking than a clutch of smaller ones in disparate materials.

PICK THE PERFECT POT

Choose a material that suits your style and the place where the containers are to reside. It might seem boring to stick to one particular type, but be wary of using too many different materials. That can produce a scrappy effect, even though they may have cost you dearly!

Terracotta

Clay containers help to keep roots cool and they look especially appropriate in cottage gardens or where you're growing herbs and Mediterranean plants. They vary in the shade of orange, from bright to pale and dusky. Check they are frost-proof (and note, frost-resistant doesn't mean frost-proof!), otherwise they may crack and crumble in icy weather.

Metal

Galvanised tubs and tanks look great filled with vegetables, fruit trees and spring bulbs such as tulips and daffodils. The galvanising will prolong their life but they may still start to deteriorate after five years or so. That said, they seem to suit almost any garden. Keep them off the ground on 'pot feet' to extend their use, and bear in mind they can get hot in the summer.

Stone troughs

Brilliant for alpine plants and ferns. Raise them up on stone or brick piers to give them most impact and be prepared to pay a considerable amount of money. Still, they'll last forever and be the envy of your friends. Just remember that they are extremely weighty.

Glazed pots

Blue glazed pots were all the rage 20-odd years ago but can look a bit passé now. Nevertheless, individual glazed pots can look dramatic when planted up with a single small tree. It's worth noting that if the neck of the pot is smaller than its waist, it'll be nigh on impossible to extract a mature tree or shrub from its confines without having to break the container.

Wooden crates and wicker baskets

These look great filled with all manner of plants, but to make them last longer it's best to use them as 'cache pots' (outer covers), hiding simple plastic pots inside. If in direct contact with compost, they'll rot rapidly. You could use circular wicker baskets as covers for large black plastic pots and bring the baskets indoors in winter.

Polystone

A relatively new and long-lasting material, made from a mix of ground-up stone and recycled plastic. Available in many styles and shapes and hugely durable, they're generally good value and chic where a modern effect is required.

CHOOSING PLANTS AND COMPOST

When it comes to choosing your plants, bear in mind you can actually grow anything in a container – trees, shrubs, perennials and more – but just be aware of the likely restrictions in terms of growth: an oak tree can be grown a large pot, but only for a few years before it needs a move.

Compost choice is important too – peat-free multi-purpose compost is ideal for annuals and bedding, while perennials and larger plants prefer a soil-based mix, again peat-free, which offers more weight for stability and provides nutrients for longer. Just remember to put large containers in their final position before filling them. Sounds obvious, but it's easily overlooked.

HOW TO PLANT A
SUMMER CONTAINER

 30 MINUTE TASK
BEST TIME TO DO: JUNE

You will need:
– Chaste tree (*Vitex agnus-castus*)
– *Verbena rigida*
– Red fountain grass (*Pennisetum advena* 'Rubrum')
– Peat-free multi-purpose compost
– Terracotta pot, approximately 45cm diameter

1. Check there are drainage holes in your container – if not, drill several. Place it in the position where you want to display it. Then half-fill it with peat-free compost. Prepare your plants by watering really well.

2. Experiment with positioning your plants while they're still in their pots. It's generally best to put taller ones at the back or centre to provide focal interest, then arrange smaller plants around them to create a good balance.

3. Once you're happy with your arrangement, remove each plant from its pot and lightly loosen its roots if possible. Then put them back in their final positions, turning each plant so its best side faces outward.

4. Backfill with compost, ensuring there are no gaps around the roots, as you gently firm the plants in. Water thoroughly after planting, then keep the compost just moist. For summer displays, after six weeks start adding a liquid feed to your watering regime.

SPRING
Perfect for smaller pots

Grasses and bulbs are made for each other, reminiscent of wild hedgerows where they bob about in the slightest breeze, making everything feel fresh and spring-like. Mexican feather grass is just the right size for a small pot, while the aqua-blue pansies and grape hyacinths add a splash of colour.

You will need:
– Mexican feather grass (*Stipa tenuissima*) x 1
– *Muscari* 'Blue Magic' x 3
– Yellow and purple pansies x 5
– *Euonymus japonicus* 'Microphyllus Variegatus' x 1
– 40cm long galvanised metal trough

AUTUMN
Shady showstopper

This pot brings a light, fresh feel with its shades of cheery pink. The magenta alstroemeria and dusky double-flowered anemone will both bloom into November, while the bold, spiky foliage of the cordyline adds year-round shades of warm purple and shocking pink in each dagger-shaped leaf. All these plants enjoy moisture and light shade. For a similar effect, try a pink echinacea, pink dahlia and *Scabiosa* 'Raspberry Sorbet'.

You will need:
– Japanese anemone (*Anemone* x *hybrida* 'Pretty Lady Julia') x 1
– *Cordyline* 'Pink Passion' x 1
– *Alstroemeria* 'Princess Louise' x 1
– Approximately 30cm terracotta pot

WINTER
Winter flowering wonder

With nodding blooms and dusky backs to the petals, this hellebore looks as if it is spangled with a light frost. The bronze sedge and wood spurge stems pick out tones from the hellebore stalks, while pretty, pink winter-flowering heathers soften the scheme. This pot will stay looking good over many weeks, positioned on the corner of a sunny patio where it can be enjoyed from the house.

You will need:
– Leatherleaf sedge (*Carex buchananii*)
– Wood spurge (*Euphorbia amygdaloides* 'Purpurea')
– Heather (*Erica carnea*)
– *Helleborus* x *sahinii* 'Winterbells'
– Approximately 40cm terracotta pot

10 FOOLPROOF PLANTS FOR POTS

○ Heuchera (year-round foliage)
○ Skimmia (winter berries)
○ Carex (year round)
○ Hellebores (winter/early spring flowers)
○ Wallflowers (spring colour)
○ Nemesia (summer colour)
○ Pelargoniums (summer flowering)
  – pictured above
○ Lavender (summer colour)
○ Pansies (winter or summer bedding)
○ Petunias (summer and autumn flowering bedding)

HOW TO PLANT UP A HANGING BASKET

30 MINUTE TASK

BEST TIME TO DO: APRIL–JUNE

You will need:
– Hanging basket and liner
– Peat free, multi-purpose compost
– Soil based compost
– Granular plant food
– Bucket
– Mix of trailing and upright plants

Add height and potentially hundreds of colourful flowers to your garden with a few hanging baskets. Traditional hanging basket plants include trailing petunias, lobelias and tuberous begonias, which can keep flowering until the end of autumn. They won't tolerate frost, so stand your planted basket on a bucket and keep it in a greenhouse or well-lit porch for a week or two after planting, before hanging it up after the last frosts.

Many summer-flowering hanging basket plants need frequent watering, so it can help to add water-retaining crystals to the compost or use drought-resistant plants such as trailing sedums, calibrachoas, pelargoniums or osteospermums.

Use a peat-free multi-purpose compost with some slow-release granular plant food, and add in a couple of handfuls of soil-based compost, too, to help retain moisture. Ideally, keep the compost indoors for a few days before planting so it's warm for the plants' roots.

1. Add a liner so that it fits the basket well, then cut holes for trailing plants. Make them a bit on the small side – compost will fall out if they are too wide.

2. Place your basket on a bucket, unhook the chain and fill it one-third full with compost. Then feed your trailing plants through the planting holes.

3. Add more compost, then put in the other plants. Ensure that their rootballs are not touching the side. Firm in each plant well and cover with extra compost.

4. Water well, repeating if it's dry. Hang the basket up in a sunny spot for flowering plants. Plants grown more for their foliage can be grown in some shade.

Container care tips

Once you have successfully planted up your container, make sure you are giving the plants within it the correct care for long-term success.

○ Water containers thoroughly morning or evening, so that the compost is given a good soaking. Twice-daily watering may be needed in the height of summer if the weather is especially warm and dry. Set up an automatic irrigation system if you're unlikely to find the time to water regularly.

○ Give all plants in containers a dilute liquid feed every week or ten days from June to September. Organic tomato feed is good for anything that flowers or fruits.

○ Protect any pots that aren't frost-proof by wrapping them in bubble polythene over winter or moving them close to the house wall.

○ When plants outgrow their containers, move them into larger pots in spring rather than summer or autumn. Once shrubs or trees outgrow your largest container, recognise that it's time to move them into the ground or, if you have no available space, give them away.

Focus on boundaries

When garden space is limited and every piece of ground is planted, the only way is up! Vertical gardening is the ultimate space-saver for compact plots, providing maximum impact from a small or non-existent footprint.

Flanking tall walls with year-round interest calls for a range of climbing plants, but these rampant scramblers are just a small element of a palette. There are trailing plants, herbs, fan-trained fruit trees and quick-fix annuals that can all play their part in sending the garden skyward.

Walls provide a great growing environment with their potential for heat retention and expanses of unused space, but beware: lofty landscapes can be tricky without the right planning. While walls retain heat, thus allowing tender species to thrive, this also means that pots dry out more quickly.

There is also the issue of rain shadow, where the soil below walls is often powder dry. Counter all these issues with careful plant selection and diligent watering, or set up an automatic drip-irrigation system.

So, make the most of your walls and get growing vertically. Fences and walls can be planted with climbers such as clematis and roses that will bring colour through summer without taking up extra border space. Alternatively you could use your boundaries to grow veg such as runner or French beans. There are climbers for every season. Mix a late-flowering clematis with a winter clematis and evergreen jasmine and you'll have something attractive to look at all year.

TOP PLANT PICKS FOR BOUNDARIES

- Espalier fruit trees
- Climbing honeysuckle
- *Clematis armandii* (spring flowering clematis)
- *Clematis cirrhosa* (winter flowering – try 'Wisley Cream')
- *Clematis viticella* (summer flowering clematis – try 'Madame Julia Correvon')
- Star jasmine, *Trachelospermum jasminoides* (good for an east- or west-facing boundary)
- Climbing roses such as *Rosa* 'New Dawn' or 'Constance Spry'
- Passionflower (*Passiflora caerulea*)
- Chocolate vine (*Akebia quinata*) (fast growing, semi-evergreen coverage)
- Pyracantha – train against a wall for autumn berries and flowers in late spring

Below: Star jasmine has scented flowers from mid to late summer

Above: Ivy provides year-round evergreen coverage for boundaries

Left: Repeat-flowering, climbing roses like *Rosa* 'Pippin' add colour to boundaries

PLANTING DOS

○ Check your container drains well – it must have one or more drainage holes in the base that are large enough to allow excess water to escape. Keep the holes from getting blocked with compost by adding a couple of inches of gravel in the base of the container. Avoid using other materials, which can block the holes.

○ Pick a style that suits your property – laser-cut steel is not country cottage, while a native hedge is.

○ Ensure the height and position of any boundary allows you privacy from neighbours. This may involve planting pleached trees in front of a hedge, fence or wall to increase the height and, therefore, privacy.

○ If you are in a wind-prone area opt for hedges rather than walls or fences.

○ Consider the width of your boundary and how much garden space you are willing to sacrifice.

○ Give plants a through watering both before and after planting. Then continue watering regularly throughout the growing season.

○ Position plants at the same depth they were growing previously. With shrubs and trees, ensure the soil mark on the stem is level with the surface of the compost.

○ Leave a gap between the surface of the compost and the rim of the pot to allow for watering – at least 5cm in large containers.

○ Raise the pot off the ground on bricks or pot feet to ensure water drains out easily, especially in winter. This will also prolong the life of containers made from perishable materials such as wood.

○ Choose whether to add a mulch – a topping of gravel looks very attractive, but can also make it a bit more difficult to see if the plants need watering.

○ Keep long-term plantings thriving by replacing the uppermost 5cm of compost each spring. Adding a good handful of blood, fish and bonemeal will give them a boost, too.

PLANTING DON'TS

○ Avoid using garden soil in containers – it won't drain well enough and may contain pests. Instead use peat-free multi-purpose compost for temporary (seasonal) plantings and a mixture of this and soil-based John Innes No.2 potting compost for plants that will stay in the container for longer than a year.

○ Do not exceed a height of 1.8m if you are creating solid boundaries, such as walls or fences. This is the limit set by most local councils. If you are seeking a higher boundary than 1.8m, opt for a hedge, but be aware that you could fall foul of a 'right to light' claim from a neighbour.

○ Don't waste money on cheap fence panels – these can be a false economy as they need replacing often.

Left: Ajuga, brunnera and *Tiarella* 'Iron Butterfly' are a good combination for shade

Actions:
– Plant up a container
– Choose some climbers to transform your boundary

CHAPTER SIX

Grow what you love to eat

Grow what you love to eat

Left: Runner beans
and onions grow well
in a sunny spot

There is a lot written about the flavour, tenderness and freshness of home-grown produce, but the real reward is the sense of satisfaction and achievement. There can be frustrations when growing your own food – from pests and diseases to droughts and frosts. The trick is to try and reduce the chances of things going wrong. Any garden can produce vegetables, whatever its size, provided the conditions are right and aspirations are tailored to circumstances. Where space is at a premium, salads can be grown in pots and window boxes, and tomatoes in hanging baskets.

To increase the likelihood of getting a decent harvest, you need to give the plants themselves the best possible chance of doing well. There are two important things to remember: first, only grow crops that you enjoy eating. Obvious? Only perhaps after you've sown a row of every possible veg in a fit of early spring passion, then found that half of them have run to seed because no one in the family likes eating them. If you limit what you grow, there will be more time to look after your crops.

The second thing to remember is to ensure that no crop goes short of water. Dryness at the roots will bring growth to a halt and may cause plants to run to seed. Evenly moist earth is the best way to ensure success with all vegetables.

If you have space, there are also many types of fruit that are easy for beginners to try. Sometimes fruit can be easier to grow – strawberries and raspberries will produce a harvest every year, with little maintenance. Perennials herbs, too, require little work once planted and will keep you in pickings year round.

Core skills:
– Chitting potatoes
– Plant a fruit tree
– Plant a herb container

5 steps to success

1. **Try to match the size of your plot to the time available.** Don't take on a huge area full of weeds if you only have a couple of spare hours at weekends. If you're busy, just start small. Vegetables don't need much fuss, but they do need consistent attention. Half an hour after work each day is enough – though you'll probably find yourself still there much later, as growing veg is moreish.

2. **When you're just beginning, success is all-important,** so stick to easy crops that give rich rewards, such as runner beans, courgettes, potatoes, salads and onions from sets. Avoid trickier crops, such as Florence fennel or cauliflowers, until you're more experienced.

3. **The more limited your space,** the more important it is to grow the vegetables you like best. So make a list of your favourites, then work out how they could grow together, and get sowing. In fact, you don't even need a garden – just a few pots.

4. **While some crops grow best on particular soils** (brassicas are best in alkaline soils and carrots love deep sandy soil), vegetables will actually grow in any soil. But soil is alive and should be nurtured and managed lovingly. When we grow vegetables, we ask a lot of it, so we must be prepared to do our bit to replace what we take out. Adding compost in spring and autumn (homemade is best, but shop-bought is fine) and well-rotted manure will help maintain soil fertility.

5. **Always choose a sunny spot for your veg patch.** Most crops will grow far better when they do not have to struggle for light. Pick a south-facing spot, ideally with a hedge giving shelter from strong winds. Leafy crops will tolerate shade, so don't despair if your garden is mainly shady, but where possible make the most of the sun.

Right: Crops such as courgettes and sweetcorn thrive in sunny veg beds

Where to grow?

Left: Tomatoes need full
sun to grow well and ripen
before the end of summer

Doing a bit of legwork upfront will save time once the growing season gets under way.

○ A raised bed eliminates time-consuming problems from the outset as you can fill it with good topsoil and keep weeds at bay from the off.

○ Make sure it is accessible from all sides – good access makes sowing, planting and harvesting quick and easy.

○ Pick a sunny and sheltered spot that gets shade for some of the day – the shade will help to reduce time spent watering.

○ Aim to position your plot near an outside tap or water butt as this will save time spent having to lug cans of water around.

○ If you're growing in the ground, avoid areas with lots of perennial weeds – keeping on top of them will take too much time.

○ If you choose to grow in pots, make sure you have time to water them every day.

Types of veg to grow

FRUITING VEGETABLES

Where to grow
Tomatoes and cucumbers need full sun to do well, while marrows and courgettes can cope with a little shade but not dense gloom. All enjoy free-draining soil that has been enriched with well-rotted compost or manure. Tomatoes can cope with slightly poorer soil than courgettes, which like it really rich. Pumpkins need the richest of all, growing happily in pure manure, relishing its ample supplies of nutrients and moisture.

Getting started
Don't rush. These are tender plants that will shrivel if planted out too soon. Wait until the weather is warming up before you sow, and ensure all risk of frost is passed before you plant them out – the end of May in most places – and they'll soon romp away and overtake plants set out earlier.

Problem solving

Poor weather is the greatest enemy of these plants and low temperatures will affect fruit development – especially in courgettes. With tomatoes, make sure you know if you're growing a bush variety or a single-stem type that will need sideshoots removing. Both kinds will benefit from staking. Tomatoes will develop sunken black areas on the underside of the fruits (blossom end rot) when watering is erratic.

If space is really tight, tomatoes are worth growing in tubs, hanging baskets (the bushy, cherry types) and growing bags. Don't be greedy – settle for three trusses of fruit and you'll stand more chance of them ripening outdoors in an English summer. Peppers and aubergines are always a gamble outdoors – a greenhouse will produce more reliable crops.

ONION FAMILY

Where to grow
They like sun and rich, really well-drained soil.

Getting started
Seeds can be sown early in the year under glass, or outdoors once the soil has warmed up a little. However, sets (small onions) are an easier option.

Below left: Onions are easy to grow from sets

Below right: Maincrop potatoes can be harvested from late August to October

Problem solving

Plant onion sets so they're buried just beneath the soil surface (if you leave the tips sticking out, blackbirds will uproot them). Space the rows far enough apart to take a Dutch hoe – onions don't like competition from weeds, so regular hoeing is essential. Never let them go short of water – if they do, they'll stop swelling and probably start flowering. At harvesting time, leave the bulbs on the soil surface to ripen in the sun so that they store for longer. With spring onions, don't sow too many in one go – sow a short row every three or four weeks from April onwards. That way you'll be able to harvest a succession of tender and tasty young plants.

ROOT CROPS

Where to grow

Sow in soil that was manured for a previous crop. Freshly manured ground will attract slugs to potato tubers and can sometimes encourage the roots of carrots, parsnips and radishes to fork. Parsnips can tolerate some shade, but good light will allow foliage to produce more food to send below ground.

Getting started

Parsnips were traditionally among the earliest crops sown, but even they are best committed to the earth when it has warmed up a little. Early seed potatoes are best sprouted (chitted) on a sunny windowsill before planting to speed up the growing process, but with maincrop spuds this isn't really necessary.

Problem solving

Don't let them go short of water – it slows down or stops growth and makes the roots of carrots and parsnips turn woody; potatoes will stop swelling. With carrots, sow sparsely to avoid thinning out the seedlings, as this releases a strong aroma that attracts carrot fly. Also use insect-proof mesh to keep them away. Pest- and disease-resistant varieties are always worth growing.

BRASSICAS

Where to grow

Brassicas (cabbages, cauliflowers, broccoli, Brussels sprouts and similar) like lots of light. Remember, too, that they need firm ground – you're likely to get weaker plants if your soil is light and fluffy.

Getting started

It's always worth starting them off in a seed bed in summer or in seed trays in a greenhouse in spring, then planting them outdoors at the final spacing when they're 10–15cm high. When transplanting, dig holes for your young plants and fill them with water before planting. Then firm in the plants. 'Puddling them in' like this will help make sure their roots are in good contact with the soil. F1 hybrid varieties will grow with more vigour and many will offer greater resistance to disease.

Problem solving
Club root will stunt brassicas, leading to poor results, so avoid growing them in affected sites. This fungal disease is more prevalent in acidic soils with poor drainage, so deter it by adding lime to reduce acidity, and improve drainage with sharp sand and grit.

In summer, cover plants with fine mesh netting to keep off cabbage white butterflies; in winter use wider mesh netting to protect from pigeons. Put felt collars round stem bases to deter cabbage root fly.

Keep down weeds, which can harbour pests and diseases, and avoid disturbing the shallow roots of brassicas with the hoe. Stake top-heavy Brussels sprouts in winter.

BEANS AND PEAS

Where to grow
Ideally, these need full sun and rich well-drained soil that isn't likely to dry out too rapidly in summer. Runner beans can be grown in a large tub up a wigwam of canes, but remember to water them frequently.

Getting started
Never sow the seeds in cold, wet ground. Broad beans are quite tough, but French and runner beans will most likely rot. Wait for warmer weather or sow under cover in small pots and plant out when the weather warms up.

Problem solving
Peas and beans are greedy, so enrich the soil with lots of well-rotted compost and manure. Over winter, dig a trench where runner beans are going to grow and gradually fill it with all kinds of moisture-retaining material, from compost and manure to torn-up newspaper. The plants will appreciate the reservoir. With peas and beans, keeping the soil moist is the key to good growth – if it dries out, they will stop growing, flowering and cropping. You could also apply a mulch of compost over the root area in June, to help conserve moisture.

Aside from cold, wet earth at sowing time, mice can be another major issue, eating the seeds before they germinate. Sowing in pots and planting out later makes it easier to defend your seeds.

Always harvest the pods when young, before they have a chance to become stringy. You may need to net pea plants to protect them from birds.

Above left: Pak choi 'Rubi'

Above right: A variety of cos and curly-leaved lettuces

LEAFY VEGETABLES

Where to grow
They like sun or part shade, in soil that contains a reasonable amount of organic matter. Salad crops such as lettuces and rocket are perfect for growing in containers.

Getting started
Start sowing when the ground has warmed up, but avoid sowing during really hot spells and when the soil is likely to dry out. With fast-growing leafy crops such as lettuces, it's best to sow in small batches – a 1m row every couple of weeks – otherwise much of the crop will go to waste.

Problem solving
For even growth, they need consistently moist soil and temperatures that don't fluctuate greatly. Very hot or cold weather is likely to lead to crop failure. Look out for varieties that are resistant to diseases such as mildew. Cover with insect-proof mesh to keep out leaf-eating pests such as flea beetles.

5 easy crops for a beginner

Courgettes

These easy veg are trouble-free, germinate quickly and one or two plants will give you more than enough crops to last all summer. They do need plenty of space. If you're growing a courgette in a pot, choose a compact variety. You can sow indoors and then plant them out once the danger of frost is over, or wait and sow outdoors in late May or early June. They need rich soil and plenty of water. Harvest when the fruits are no bigger than 10cm for the tastiest crops.

Sow indoors: April–June | *Plant:* May–June | *Harvest:* July–October

Beetroot

Choose a bolt resistant variety like 'Boltardy' and this veg shouldn't cause any problems. You can sow direct when the soil warms up, which means you don't have to look after seedlings indoors. Sow the seeds thinly, 10cm apart in 2.5cm deep rows.

Sow: March–July | *Harvest:* June–October

Climbing French beans

French beans are heavy croppers and will produce beans over a long period if you keep picking them. Sow indoors and plant out once the danger of frost is over in May or June. They are also easy to sow outdoors. Grow in the ground or containers. There are dwarf types available if you're short on space.

Sow: April–July | *Harvest:* June–October

Salad leaves

These are quick to crop and make a great pick for beginners. You don't need much space and growing your own will save money on buying the supermarket bags. Sow every few weeks to keep your crops coming. You should get a harvest in around six weeks. This crop is perfect for pots or small vegetable plots.

Sow: March–September | *Harvest:* January–December

Early potatoes

It's very satisfying to grow your own potatoes. You can grow them in portable sacks on balconies or patios, or in the ground if you have space. For bags, plant them in 15cm of multi-purpose compost in an old compost sack. As they grow roll up the sides of the bag and keep burying the stems with more compost; you'll have a crop ready within 10–12 weeks.

Plant: March–April | *Harvest:* June–July

Clockwise from top left: Harvesting beetroot; container-grown courgettes; salad leaves; harvesting main crop potatoes; climbing bean 'Blauhilde'

HOW TO CHIT POTATOES

You will need:
- First early potatoes
- Egg box

A short row of first earlies can be fitted into most gardens to produce tasty new potatoes. The earliest crops come from seed potatoes (raised specifically to be healthy and virus free) that are chitted before being planted.

The word chit dates from the seventeenth century and means 'a shoot', so chitting is the act of encouraging seed potatoes to sprout before they are planted. This is done because if they are given a head start and planted with young shoots that are already growing they are likely to produce a crop sooner than if planted totally dormant. This means that you can be enjoying your new potatoes earlier than if they had not sprouted at all. It's very easy, and

once the shoots are 2–3cm long the potatoes can be planted out, safe in the knowledge that growth is underway.

1. Don't bother chitting maincrop varieties, which stay in the ground longer. Chit first and and second early varieties (the quickest to mature).

2. Examine each tuber - you'll find more tiny buds, or eyes, on one end. Stand tubers in an egg box, in a bright, frost-free place, eyes up, to sprout.

3. Start them off in February as it will take several weeks for shoots to grow.

4. Rub off excess shoots, leaving three or four per tuber - they should be about an inch long. Leave too many shoots per tuber and you'll get a lot of tiny spuds on each plant.

No time? Try plug plants

Once upon a time, seed companies just sold seeds, but now their catalogues are full of young 'plug' plants (so named because they're raised individually in modules in seed trays). The great advantage of these young plants is that they've come through their infancy and already have a good root system. If you plant them spaced the right distance apart, they're almost bound to grow.

However, while they are time-saving, they're also expensive, and they take away some of the thrill of growing from seed. But they are very handy when you want to plant crops regularly to provide a non-stop supply (known as succession planting). As soon as one crop is finished, the next can be put in the ground to replace it, already half-grown.

There is no reason why you shouldn't grow your own plug plants. Suitable module trays are cheap and, after a wash, can be reused for years. First sow your seeds in a regular seed tray – try cabbages, sweetcorn or beetroot – spacing them a centimetre or two apart. Then, once they've germinated and sprouted their first or second pair of leaves, carefully transfer each seedling into its own compartment of the module tray. You can use a pencil to help lift the plants, supporting their roots, from one tray to the other. And don't worry, you don't need a greenhouse – just put them on a warm, sunny windowsill until they're large enough to plant out in the vegetable plot.

Success with fruit

Fruit is probably the scariest aspect of gardening: all that pruning to maintain shape and to encourage regular cropping, and those mysterious rootstocks with their strange letters and numbers, one to which the cultivated varieties are grafted – a dark art if ever there was one. The best thing to do is start slowly with a few of the easy to grow fruits. Edge your way into the world of fruit growing and find it rewarding rather than daunting, even in a small garden.

The easiest things to grow are raspberries and strawberries – 'soft fruits', as distinct from 'top fruit', which grows on trees. Strawberries demand nothing more than a decent patch of well-drained earth in full sun. In shade, they will sulk and in soggy ground they will rot. A strawberry bed, once planted (and netted to protect it from birds when the fruits are ripening) should yield well for three years. After that, the plants start to lose their vigour and need to be replaced with new plants. Strawberries can also be grown in pots.

Raspberries are also easy – either the summer-fruiting varieties, which produce their crop on one-year-old canes, or the autumn fruiters, which carry the berries on canes produced that year. Pruning is simple with either. The old canes of summer fruiters are cut out at ground level after the crop has been picked. The new canes that have sprung up that year, among the old ones, should be retained, spaced out and tied into a post-and-wire framework – they will bear next year's fruit. With autumn-fruiting varieties (which can be picked from September onwards), all canes are cut right back to ground level in winter. You don't even need to stake them if you don't want to – they are self-supporting and should crop well every year, though they'll need to be disciplined from taking over the veg patch – make sure to dig up any suckers that emerge among other crops.

5 easy fruit to grow

Strawberries
This is a great crop to grow in pots. You can fit around three plants in a 30cm container and the bonus of this is that they are out of reach of hungry slugs. They can also be used to edge borders. Bare-root plants will produce flowers and fruit within about 60 days, or you can buy potted plants at the garden centre. Good varieties include 'Honeoye', which is very hardy and early fruiting, or 'Cambridge Favourite', which is known for its flavour.

Plant: March–May | *Harvest:* May–September

Blueberries

These shrubs are perfect for small gardens because they thrive in pots of ericaceous compost. Not only do these plants offer sweet summer berries, but they also have spring flowers and striking autumn colour. When planting a large blueberry shrub, use a pot that is at least 45cm in diameter; 60cm if you have space.

Plant: January–December | *Harvest:* July–September

Raspberries

The easiest raspberries to grow are autumn-fruiting varieties as the pruning is simple – cut them down to the ground after fruiting. They are also more compact plants and can be grown in containers. For pots, try 'Autumn Treasure'. If you have more space, try summer fruiting varieties such as 'Glen Ample'. The cheapest way to buy raspberry plants is to order bare-root canes.

Plant: October–April | *Harvest:* June–October

Rhubarb

For an early fruit crop, rhubarb is the one to grow. Plant the crowns in winter and don't harvest any stems in the first year. This will allow plants to build up their strength so they can cope with regular harvesting the next year. Pull the stems rather than cut them. Plant in sun or partial shade, in rich, moist soil.

Plant: November–February | *Harvest:* March–July

Apples

Apples are one of the easiest tree fruits to grow. For a small garden, choose an apple tree that has a dwarfing rootstock (ask for dwarfing M26 – this means it won't grow to more than 2m tall). Standard trees can be grown in a large container – choose a self-fertile variety such as 'James Grieve'. You should use a container that is at least 50cm in diameter.

Plant: November–March | *Harvest:* September–November

HOW TO PLANT FRUIT TREES IN A POT

30–60 MINUTE TASK

BEST TIME TO DO: NOVEMBER–MARCH

You will need:
– Large pot (at least 45cm)
– Peat-free, loam-based compost
– Apple tree on a dwarfing rootstock
– Tree tie
– Stake
– Mulch (optional)

Site your tree in the sun and find a pot that's at least 45cm in diameter. Pot the tree in situ as it will be really heavy to move around. It's best to plant between autumn and spring for the tree to establish well, but container-grown trees can be planted at other times if you avoid hot weather.

Help the tree establish good roots by using mycorrhizal fungi – these occur naturally in soil but won't be in your fresh new compost. Soak the tree roots, then put the powdered fungi on the roots before potting.

Keep the tree well watered and, once it is established, it will need light pruning. Refresh the top layer of compost and add fertiliser each spring.

1. Choose a large pot to give your tree the best possible conditions, then part fill with a good quality loam-based potting compost.

2. Handle the tree by the rootball or stem base to avoid damaging the graft union. Place in the centre and press more compost firmly around the roots.

3. Ensure the top of the tree's rootball is at the same level as the new compost. Push in a stake and attach using a tree tie. Apply a mulch of organic matter or decorative stone, keeping it away from the trunk.

4. Fill a can with water and drench the pot. Even if water runs out at the bottom, there may be areas of compost that haven't soaked up the water, so use plenty.

Growing your own herbs

Left: A raised bed is an attractive planter for herbs and makes picking them easier

Herbs tick all the boxes for people interested in creating a better lifestyle for themselves and their families. They're tasty, healthy and popular with keen cooks and food lovers – even when they're non-gardeners. Herbs are also an easy first step into gardening – lots of people who begin with a pot of supermarket herbs on a windowsill soon progress to a veg plot, a greenhouse, the whole nine yards.

The great thing is that most of the popular culinary herbs are productive and easy to grow. And they aren't just for 'everyday' pasta sauces and casseroles. Once you grow a good range at home, you can make all sorts of tasty herbal treats, from lavender jelly to rosemary-infused olive oil or tarragon vinegar, plus herby breads and biscuits.

Pots of supermarket herbs are a good starting point, but there's a limited range and they've been 'factory farmed', with controlled lighting, temperature and humidity levels to maximise fast growth. This means they'll do well on a kitchen windowsill, but don't put them outside, as the shock may kill them.

Once you start using lots of herbs, it's more economical to grow your own. Several popular kinds are easily raised from seed – not just the 'big three' from supermarkets (parsley, basil and coriander), but also desirables like pot marjoram, chervil and dill. With these, make several sowings each season so you always have some at the right stage to snip.

Perennial herbs are best bought as small plants in the outdoor herb section of a garden centre. More unusual kinds can be tracked down at specialist herb farms. When buying, choose strong, healthy young plants with a neat, bushy shape. Once you have a plant, you can propagate more – by dividing mints, tarragon and chives, and by taking cuttings of thyme, sage and rosemary, and of novelties like edible French lavender, lemon verbena and scented-leaved pelargoniums.

Growing herbs in pots is easy. Most perennials prefer soil-based John Innes compost, and for Mediterranean herbs add 10 per cent potting grit to this to improve drainage. Multi-purpose compost is usually best for annual herbs, especially those you replace several times per season. Terracotta pots are traditional, but herbs also do well in plastic, ceramic or wooden containers.

Keep big or large-spreading herbs, plus those that have rather specialised needs, in individual pots of their own, as it makes them easier to manage. Basil, for instance, needs warmth, shelter and very careful watering. But there are lots you can group together in communal containers, such as strawberry planters, which are like Ali Baba jars with planting pockets in the sides, and herb planters, which are similar but several sizes smaller (and frankly often a tad too small). Tubs are good too – a 30–45cm wide tub is ideal for three perennial or five annual herbs, but choose those that enjoy the same growing conditions.

As a general rule, you can group together Mediterranean herbs (the evergreen shrubby kind that like lots of sun and good drainage), OR the more traditional English cottage-garden herbs, such as chives, mint, tarragon, parsley, chervil and sorrel. The latter like more moisture-retentive conditions and good light but not strong midday summer sun.

3 EASY HERBS

Basil
Basil is easy to grow from seed yourself. Either keep your plants on a sunny windowsill or plant out in a warm, sunny spot once the risk of frost is over. Don't let plants dry out but don't overwater, especially at night when the water is absorbed less quickly. Pick leaves little and often from the top, to create a bushy plant.

Sow: February–April | *Plant:* June–July | *Harvest:* June–September

Thyme
Perfect for pots and borders, thyme is a useful herb to having at hand for cooking. It's perennial and offers pickings year round. It also has pretty flowers in the summer – pink, purple or white – depending on which variety you grow. Plant in free-draining soil, in a sunny spot.

Plant: March–May / September–November | *Harvest:* year round

Chives
Buy a plant from the garden centre or supermarket and plant out for years of pickings as your plant will resprout each spring. They are very easy to grow and cause no trouble. Cut off the flowering stems to encourage new leaves. You can add the flowers to salads.

Sow: March–May | *Plant:* April–June | *Harvest:* July–September

Right: Chives in flower

Below: Thyme makes a
good container plant

Left: Thai basil has red
stems and a spicier flavour
than normal basil

3 great combinations for your herb pots

When planting several herbs together in one pot, make sure they all like the same conditions. Here are some ideal trios for a 30cm pot:

FOR SEMI-SHADE

Parsley, chives, Eau de Cologne mint

These three culinary herbs have attractively contrasting leaves, and the chives also have edible mauve flowers. Chives can also be grown in full sun, but will grow well in dappled or partial shade. Eau de Cologne mint is smaller and less rampant than the better-known apple mint or spearmint. It's delightfully scented and great for mint sauce or for boiling with new potatoes or peas. It also repels flies.

Aftercare: Plant this trio into peat-free John Innes No. 2 or 3 compost, then water and feed regularly. Each spring, tip the pot out and refill with fresh compost, replace the parsley with new plants raised from seed, and divide the chives and mint, replanting the best bits.

FOR FULL SUN

Rosemary, thyme, oregano

Pretty enough for a patio or sunny window box, these will all flower and attract bees. Use gritty, soil-based compost and stand the pot on feet to improve drainage, particularly in winter.

Aftercare: Clip the plants after flowering to tidy them up and encourage new leafy shoots; rosemary may need harder pruning to stop it getting too big. The plants will be happy in the pot for several years if you top dress with fresh John Innes No. 3 compost each spring and feed regularly over the summer. When the plants get woody, take cuttings and use to create a new display.

COOKS' CHOICE

Basil, leaf coriander, chervil

These three are key ingredients in many cooked dishes, as well as a great addition to salads.

Aftercare: use multi-purpose compost and take care with watering – these plants don't like being waterlogged or getting too dry. Stand the pot in good light but avoid strong midday sun. Grow several batches of these herbs from seed over the season and replant the pot once the original residents have been heavily cut or when they start trying to flower.

5 tips for keeping herbs productive

RE-SOW ANNUALS AND BIENNIALS

To ensure you have a steady supply of fresh plants for your pots, sow a new batch once you're halfway through using your current crop. Sprinkle the seeds thinly over the surface of a pot of multi-purpose compost, and don't bother pricking out the seedlings. In winter, sow into pots on a warm windowsill.

PROVIDE THE RIGHT CONDITIONS

Mediterranean herbs love lots of sun and good drainage. More traditional British herbs, such as parsley, mint and chives, plus tarragon and leaf coriander, enjoy lots of light but get stunted or tough if too dry, hot and sunny. Basil is fussy – grow it in good light but avoid strong midday sun and water it carefully.

RE-POT OR TOP DRESS

Give perennials a boost with fresh compost in spring. Mint needs good nourishment, so pot up a few strong roots into new compost each spring. Divide chives and tarragon every second spring, and top dress or re-pot woody Mediterranean herbs, such as rosemary, using John Innes No. 3 and a little added grit.

FEED AND WATER REGULARLY

Apply a general-purpose liquid fertiliser to keep your herbs leafy, plus an occasional dose of liquid seaweed, as the trace elements improve flavour. Adding high-potash tomato feed in mid-summer helps to toughen up Mediterranean herbs so they can withstand hot dry spells.

CUT BACK PERENNIAL HERBS ANNUALLY

Herbs that die down naturally in winter (such as mint, oregano and chives) need cutting off at ground level in late autumn to keep them tidy. They'll regrow as good as new in spring. Woody herbs (such as thyme, rosemary and sage) become straggly with age, so prune into shape after flowering or in spring. With lavender, clip it into a neat shape in late summer, removing the old flowers without cutting into old wood.

EDIBLE PLANTS DOS

○ Sow little and often to give yourself a constant supply and avoid gluts.

○ Pick vegetables young, when they're at their freshest and tastiest.

○ Rotate your crops to avoid disease and maintain vigour.

○ Use your space to the maximum – plant quick-cropping lettuces between rows of slower-growing veg such as leeks or cabbages.

○ Grow for taste rather than volume of harvest – you're not a farmer.

○ Choose an open aspect for fruit so the sun ripens stems and fruit. Avoid spots that are exposed to strong winds or low-lying areas that are frost pockets, which will lead to blossom damage and crop failure.

○ Improve the soil with a generous helping of organic matter. Improve sticky soil by adding sharp sand and grit.

○ In grass, maintain a bare area of soil 1m wide around fruit trees, to reduce competition and make feeding easier.

○ Read up about rootstocks before you buy to make sure you have the right one for your soil and space.

○ Plant bare-root fruit between November and March, but firm back any that are later loosened by winter frosts. Container-grown trees and bushes can be planted at any time of year but avoid planting during periods of drought.

EDIBLE PLANTS DON'TS

○ Never plant fruit on waterlogged ground. Good drainage is essential.

○ Don't let plants dry out completely, and feed them regularly.

○ Don't use multi-purpose compost for fruit in pots. It won't have the weight or sustenance needed for most fruits. Use a peat-free John Innes No. 3 compost. Use an ericaceous compost for blueberries.

○ Don't overcommit – only grow what you have time to look after.

Right: Small seeds can be sown indoors in trays

Jargon buster

Below: The height of raised beds makes it easier to weed and harvest veg

Chitting – encouraging potatoes to sprout before planting

Brassicas – the brassica family of vegetables includes broccoli, cauliflowers, kale and Brussels sprouts. They are nutritious and genetically similar, sharing characteristics such as being hardy and requiring fertile, well drained soil.

Transplanting – moving a seedling or plant from one place to another (such as from a small pot to the ground outdoors)

Actions:
- Choose some easy herbs, vegetables and fruit to grow
- Check the timings for each crop – when to sow or plant
- Prepare your veg patch or containers
- Start small to avoid being overwhelmed with jobs and harvests

CHAPTER SEVEN

Time it right

Time it right

Left: Leaving some areas of grass long is good for wildlife

Much of the success of tasks like pruning, lawncare and plant care depends on doing it at the right time of year. This doesn't mean that everything will go wrong if you are a couple of weeks late with mowing your lawn, but knowing the best time of year to do certain jobs makes it easier to get good results. Pruning shrubs in the wrong season can result in no flowers, while getting your lawn in good shape in spring means it will be healthier for the rest of the year.

There is no mystery to these jobs and although tasks like pruning can appear complicated, none of these techniques are difficult. It's only a matter of taking it a step at a time. The main seasons to tackle lawncare are in spring and autumn. Have a look at the guide to see what needs to be done when.

For pruning, it may seem less daunting if you write a list of the main plants in your garden that will require annual pruning – trees and shrubs – and then look up each plant to see what type of pruning it needs and when. You'll then have a good overview of what to do when and an action plan.

Core skills:
– Pruning a shrub rose
– Lawn care
– Watering correctly
– Feeding plants

5 steps to success

① **Mow regularly between April and September.** Mowing once a week, rather than once a fortnight (unless there's a drought) will help produce a thick and even lawn. It will be far less patchy than a lawn mown every two or three weeks.

② **Raise the blades between October and March** if mowing to offer the lawn more weather resistance. Even in summer, don't cut lower than half an inch. The longer the grass the more resistant it is to drought, so adjust the cutting height to an inch in prolonged dry spells.

③ **Always use the right tools.** Use secateurs for stems up to a finger's thickness, loppers on thick or tough stems (up to 3cm in diameter). For any branches thicker than this, use a pruning saw. Keep the blades of your tools clean at all times to avoid spreading infection.

④ **Keep deadheading.** Deadheading is easy and important to do in order to keep plants flowering. Once a plant has flowered, it puts it energy into setting seed. Pruning off the old flowers as soon as they fade prevents this and encourages more blooms as well as keeping plants looking their best. Roses, annuals and herbaceous perennials such as *Erysimum* 'Bowles's Mauve' are plants that will keep flowering and flowering if deadheaded.

⑤ **Water new plantings by soaking them well,** not just splashing them. Aim the water at the roots rather than the top of the plant or its leaves. This will direct water to where it's needed and avoid wasting it.

Right: Deadheading roses regularly encourages more flowers

Lawncare

Left: Keeping on top of lawncare will ensure good growth throughout the summer

A lawn is the hardest-working feature in a garden, but the one that's often the most mistreated and the most maligned. A well-kept lawn shows off beds and borders far better than paving or gravel ever can, thanks to its organic nature and its sympathetic colour and texture.

A close-mown lawn demands regular attention. Between April and September it will need cutting once a week and the clippings taken off and added to the compost heap. The edges will need regular trimming. But the results can help create a clean, uncluttered look.

Managed well, it can be beautiful in its own right and is versatile enough to suit a variety of needs and time constraints. It can be striped and manicured, allowed to grow longer at the margins or planted with wildflowers and spring bulbs, through which paths are mown. Leaving some areas of grass to grow longer will allow daisies and clover to flower, which will attract pollinators. Even a well mown lawn is more environmentally friendly than hard surfaces and a haven for all sorts of wildlife. In short, what's not to love?

LAWNCARE CALENDAR

Spring
- Mow the grass lightly in a mild March
- Grass is growing fast now, so mow once a week by April
- Lay new turf
- Sow new lawns
- Tackle weeds

Summer
- Mow once a week, except in hot, dry weather
- Raise the height of the blades in hot, dry weather and mow less frequently
- Don't let turf dry out before it has a chance to root

Autumn
- Sow new lawns in September
- Scarify in October
- Spike the lawn to improve drainage
- Apply autumn lawn feed
- Lay turf

Winter
- Stay off frosted grass, or black footprints will appear come the thaw
- Keep mowing in mild areas

MOWING

Once you're ready to cut, adjust the blades on your mower to the highest level they can go. For the first few weeks cut little and often, normally taking off no more than about a third of its height.

WATERING

Vital only on newly established lawns. Use a sprinkler attached to a hosepipe and leave it in any one spot only for half an hour. Don't water established lawns. They'll soon recover come the rains.

SCARIFYING

Every March you can rake out dead grass (thatch) and moss. Powered lawn rakes are available or you can exercise your abs with a wire-toothed rake.

EDGING

Trim the lawn edges after mowing with long-handled edging shears. It improves the appearance of the lawn and gives it a sharp profile. Once a year, re-cut the edges, ideally with a half-moon iron.

WEEDING

Lawn weedkillers are not environmentally friendly. Learn to live with a mixed sward and remove any unwanted rosette-forming weeds with a sharp knife or a daisy grubber.

REPAIRING

Worn or damaged lawn edges can be repaired by cutting out a portion of turf and reversing it so the good inside edge is turned to the outside. Bare patches can be re-seeded in spring or late summer or re-turfed at any time.

FEEDING

Use an organic feed such as blood, fish and bonemeal in spring and again in early summer. A wheeled fertiliser distributor will ensure even application and avoid using too much, saving you money.

IMPROVING DRAINAGE

Make drainage holes with a garden fork to help water escape from compacted areas. Push the fork in as deep as possible at 10cm intervals over the worst areas. You can damage the grass when frosty and make compaction worse by treading on it when wet, so wait for good weather.

Right: edge your lawn
to keep it neat

Above: Use a rake to
remove dead grass
and moss

Left: Remove lawn weeds
in the spring

Pruning

Pruning is perhaps the most overwhelming task facing any gardener – novice and enthusiast alike. This is probably because, aside from being seemingly complicated, it is impossible to stick back a part of a plant you wish you had not cut off!

But most mistakes can be rectified by time and if you know why you are pruning a particular tree or shrub before you start, then you can have in your mind a picture of what you are hoping to achieve.

Pruning comes in many forms, from simple deadheading (the removal of faded flowers to brighten up the plant and to prevent unwanted seed production), to clipping topiary specimens to create living garden sculpture, or cutting hard back to encourage more young wood.

Just make sure you are comfortable with your aims before you start and mistakes will be avoided.

WHAT IS PRUNING?

In a nutshell, pruning is the removal of part of a plant to influence its subsequent growth. Woody plants – trees and shrubs – have a clever system of growth. The 'terminal bud' – the bud at the very tip of a shoot – produces growth-inhibiting chemicals, which it passes down the stem to discourage the buds lower down from growing. This makes sure that the plant can grow upwards towards the light, where more food is to be found via photosynthesis.

If we cut off the shoot tip, no growth inhibitors are passed down the stem, with the result that the lower buds begin to grow. This is why we pinch out shoot tips, or cut them off, to encourage bushiness in all kinds of plants. So, one reason for this sort of pruning is to encourage a bushier, fuller plant, but depending on the tree or shrub in question, there are other reasons for cutting bits of it off:

○ To remove dead, diseased or damaged shoots, which would otherwise help to spread infection into healthy tissue – known as 'the three Ds'.

○ To make a plant shapelier if it has branches or shoots growing out at odd angles or where we do not want them.

○ To increase air circulation and light penetration, which will help to maintain plant health.

○ To encourage the production of a younger and more vigorous growth.

○ To remove a portion of older wood and keep a tree or shrub youthful and
    longer-lived.

○ To encourage the production of flowers and fruits, rather than leafy growth.

All of these aims can be achieved by adjusting the kind of pruning we carry
out. There is no 'one size fits all' approach, which is why pruning techniques
are often confusing. But they needn't be if your aims are clear from the outset.

GETTING TO GRIPS WITH THE BASICS

Make sure you have the right tools, and that they are clean and sharp so that
any cuts you make will be smooth. Ragged cuts will encourage fungal attack
and subsequent decay. A good pair of secateurs will cut branches up to 1cm
thick; above this, use loppers – those long-handled pruning shears. A folding
pruning saw will be handy for stems that are bigger than 3cm thick (it cuts on
the 'pull' stroke, unlike a carpenter's saw, which cuts on the 'push' stroke). A
pair of shears will be necessary for hedge and topiary clipping. Keep your
blades clean! Rub them regularly with emery paper to remove dried sap,
which will cause them to stick. If you have been cutting out diseased material,
wash them in disinfectant before oiling them ready for use next time.

Above all, have in mind what you are aiming to achieve before you start, and
an understanding of the consequences of the removal of each particular
stem. Stand back after every two or three cuts and eye up the plant. That
will help you to produce a shapely plant, which will grow in the direction you
require and produce the shoots you want to encourage.

If you are in any doubt at all, restrict your pruning to the three Ds: remove
dead, diseased and damaged stems, and leave the rest alone. As a general
rule, remember the old adage: 'Growth follows the knife.' If you cut a stem
'hard back' you will, in most cases, encourage vigorous growth. If that is what
you want (in the case of coloured-stemmed dogwoods, which are pruned
back to ground level in spring, for instance) all well and good. But consider,
instead, whether it would be better simply to thin out a plant's stems and
maybe remove just a few centimetres from the shoot tips to keep it shapely
without encouraging vigorous growth.

HOW TO MAKE THE RIGHT CUT

If you prune a plant when it's dormant, you need to know the difference
between two types of buds: flower buds and leaf buds. Knowing one from the
other is vital if your pruning is to promote optimum flowering and fruiting.
To make sure you get the timing right, make a note of when the plant flowers.
As a general rule, if it blooms from July onwards, prune in spring; if it blooms
before the end of June, prune right after flowering.

Check the colour of the stems at different times of the year too (see below),
as they respond differently to pruning depending on the season. Cutting back
young stems will promote side branching; in summer, pruning reduces vigour
and encourages flower buds; and winter pruning stimulates vigorous growth.

WHERE TO CUT

One of the key rules is to always cut back above a bud, which will then sprout to form a new stem. So look for a bud that points in the direction you want the new shoot to grow; for example, with a free-standing shrub, prune to outward-facing buds to open up the centre, but with a wall-trained shrub, cut just above buds that point out across the wall to fill any gaps, rather than out above the path where new stems would be in the way. If you can't see a bud, prune to just above a leaf joint, as the plant can produce a new shot from there.

○ Cutting too far above a bud leaves a 'snag' that will die back, potentially allowing infection to set in. This dieback will often spread down the stem, past the bud.

○ Angle your cut in the same direction that the bud is facing, so any water will run off readily. If water gets trapped around the bud, rot can set in. Cutting this way also encourages hormones to trigger the bud into growth.

○ Don't make your cut really close to the bud, as you'll damage its supporting tissues. The bud will die and infection will set in.

○ Make your cut less than a centimetre above the bud, sloping in the direction the bud is pointing, to give it the best possible chance of growing into a vigorous healthy new shoot. Always use sharp secateurs for a clean, precise cut.

Below left: Pruning wisteria in winter

Below opposite: A fan-trained peach tree

WHAT TO PRUNE WHEN

Follow this guide to make sure you're pruning at the right time of year for the best results.

Spring

- Coloured stemmed shrubs such as willows and *Cornus alba*

- Summer-flowering deciduous shrubs that flower on new growth, such as *Buddleia davidii* and French lavender

- Herbaceous perennials that have decorative seedheads or stems such as sedums and thistles

- Winter-flowering shrubs such as winter jasmine and *Viburnum* x *bodnantense*

- Most evergreens

Summer

- Tender shrubs such as abutilon and fuchsias

- Spring-flowering shrubs that flower on stems formed the previous year, such as deutzia and philadelphus

- Rhododendrons and azaleas

- Trained fruit

- Hedges such as beech, box and privet, to maintain their shape

- Fruit trees – removing soft, new growth to promote fruit formation on apples, cherries, pears and plums

Autumn

○ Summer-flowering jasmine

○ Soft and bush fruit such as summer-fruiting raspberries

○ Herbaceous perennials – untidy varieties that lack decorative seedheads such as peonies and lupins

○ Mediterranean shrubs – sun-loving shrubs that won't tolerate hard pruning in winter such as cistus and lavender

○ Yew hedges

Winter

○ Clematis – deciduous varieties that bloom in late summer such as *Clematis texensis* varieties, *Clematis viticella* varieties, and the large-flowered 'Jackmanii' group

○ Roses – while ramblers are left until summer, the following should be pruned in winter: climbing roses, floribundas, hybrid teas and species roses

○ Overgrown shrubs – deciduous shrubs such as cotinus, berberis and flowering currant often outgrow their welcome

○ Plants that bleed – woody deciduous plants that ooze sap unless pruned when dormant: acers, birches, figs and grapevines

○ Apples and pears

○ Autumn fruiting raspberries

○ Fruit bushes such as blackcurrants and gooseberries

Pruning mistakes to avoid

PRUNING TOO MUCH
If a plant is growing well, is not full of dead or diseased wood and has a pleasing shape, leave it alone. Don't butcher your plants if they are too big. Remove them completely or move them to a spot where they can grow freely and replace them with something of a more modest stature that better suits the space.

NOT PRUNING ENOUGH
Spring-flowering shrubs such as philadelphus and weigela will become congested and overcrowded with non-flowering stems if left to their own devices. Removing a few of the older branches after flowering will keep them youthful. Wisteria will run rampant if not pruned in summer to reduce the spread of those long, snaking growths. Cut them back to 30cm in July or August and in January shorten all side shoots to finger length to encourage the production of flowers.

NOT PRUNING ABOVE A NODE
Prune above a node (leaf joint) and the bud immediately below the cut – in the leaf 'axil' – will grow away well. Cut too far above the leaf joint and the stem will die back to the bud – and probably beyond, risking infection.

NOT CLEANING SECATEURS
If you have been pruning out infected tissue, there is a danger that you could spread disease to healthy plants unless your secateurs have been properly cleaned and disinfected.

NOT PRUNING AT AN ANGLE
Make your pruning cuts at an angle of 45 degrees, sloping away from the bud, to help shed water and reduce the likelihood of disease gaining a hold.

NOT REMOVING DIEBACK
If a stem is dying back, the infection can continue to advance down the stem unless that stem is cut out well back into healthy tissue.

PRUNING AT THE WRONG TIME OF YEAR
Trained fruit trees will produce more leafy growth if they are pruned in winter. Shorten the side shoots in summer and you will encourage the production of fruiting spurs, which will result in a better harvest. Plum trees, in addition, are susceptible to the debilitating fungal disease silver leaf, which is most likely to attack surfaces that are pruned in winter. So always do your pruning, if it is necessary to keep the tree shapely, in summer.

Fruit pruning

When pruning fruit trees and bushes, always use a sharp pair of secateurs and make all cuts just above an outward-facing bud with the aim of creating a cup-shaped framework with an airy, well-spaced centre.

TREE FRUIT

Remove weak or crossing stems from apple and pear trees, and shorten the main shoots by a third to produce a well-spaced framework that is fairly open in the centre.

Reduce sideshoots that are over 30cm long by half; shorter ones can be left alone.

Remove dead or dying stems, and those that are diseased, weak, rubbing on others or crossing the centre of the tree (loppers and a pruning saw will be necessary).

Avoid pruning plum trees in winter as it can encourage silver-leaf disease. If your tree crops well, and is healthy and shapely, don't get bogged down by over-elaborate pruning. Healthy, well-spaced stems and lots of fruiting sideshoots are what you need for a decent crop.

BUSH FRUIT

Prune soft-fruit bushes in winter. Cut back the main stems of gooseberries and redcurrants by approximately one third, and shorten the sideshoots growing from them to about 10cm to thin out the growth. Wall-trained fan or cordon plants should be pruned in summer.

For blackcurrants, simply cut out about a quarter of the oldest, thickest branches completely, from the base of the plant – the aim is to take out the oldest wood every year and encourage productive new shoots. If it's a large plant, cut back the tips of the remaining branches to the highest strong sideshoot.

Prune autumn-fruiting raspberries in late winter, and remember it's like the January sales – everything must go! Prune summer-fruiting varieties after harvesting, cutting out at ground level the stems that have borne fruit, and leaving the new stems to carry fruit next year.

Above: Pruning autumn raspberry canes down to the ground

Below: Winter pruning an old apple tree

HOW TO PRUNE A SHRUB ROSE

◑ 30 MINUTE TASK

BEST TIME TO DO: FEBRUARY–MARCH

You will need:
– Loppers
– Secateurs

Shrub roses are large plants that are neither 'bush' roses (floribundas or hybrid teas – the type seen in rose beds), nor climbers or ramblers. They have a naturally graceful shape, often with arching stems.

Shrub roses include species (such as *Rosa glauca*), rugosa (such as 'Roseraie de l'Hay'), damasks, bourbons and gallicas. Unlike bush roses, which are cut back hard in late winter/ early spring, shrub roses are pruned more lightly to keep the plant healthy, flowering well and a manageable size. Aim for a mix of older wood (which produces this year's flowers) and young, vigorous growth, plus good air circulation. Cutting a shrub rose back too severely will spoil its natural shape. Using a sharp tool, prune to just above a healthy bud that is pointing outwards. Make sure the cut

faces away from the bud so that rain doesn't run into it, causing it to rot.

1. Examine your plant. Look for dead stems and those that are rubbing. Use secateurs to remove these and any that are diseased. Shorten a selection of older stems to thin them out.

2. Remove a couple of older stems with loppers to encourage new shoots that will flower the following summer. Cut as close to the ground as possible (stumps encourage disease).

3. Check for old stubs where the stems were not fully cut back during the previous pruning. Remove these with secateurs to stop dieback, which can run down the stem if left in place.

4. Reduce the remaining healthy main stems by up to a third with secateurs and shorten strong side shoots to two or three buds. Mulch the plant afterwards with well-rotted manure or bark.

Plant aftercare

WATERING

You'll know from a glance at your bill that as a commodity water is not cheap, so in terms of economy you'll need to prioritise its use in the garden, reserving it for those plants that really need it, and not squandering it on those that will survive dry spells perfectly well without your watering can or hosepipe.

With a few simple precautions you'll be able to make sure your water supply is directed to those plants that will really benefit. And to avoid using mains water as much as possible, it's vital to collect and store as much rainwater as you can. Giving this to your plants will help to make this valuable resource go further.

What needs watering?

It is the plants that are most vulnerable to fluctuating moisture levels in the soil that need the most attention when it comes to watering. It stands to reason that anything growing in a container is totally at the mercy of you and your watering can. If you let the compost in pots, baskets and other containers dry out, growth stops, plants wilt and – in severe cases – they die. But if you keep the potting compost evenly moist, growth will be markedly healthier and the production of flowers and fruits more consistent.

Right: Water a row of carrots after thinning to settle the soil

Newly planted trees, shrubs, perennials and bedding plants need watering to establish their roots. They should be watered repeatedly until their root system has travelled far enough to ensure they have access to reserves deeper in the ground – generally during prolonged dry spells in their first year.

Fruit and vegetables need steady supplies of moisture to keep them growing and developing well. Take tomatoes, for instance. Allow them to dry out and growth slows down, the skin of the fruit begins to harden and when water is reapplied it has lost its flexibility and the fruit splits. It will still be edible, but nothing like as succulent as it would have been with a steady supply of moisture. Forget about watering established plants with deep root systems. Only those that have roots close to the surface and that always seem to wilt in prolonged dry spells – such as rudbeckias, phlox and asters – are worth soaking to relieve their stress and keep them growing.

Likewise, although the lawn is the first thing to suffer in a drought (grass roots being very close to the surface), it has tough little buds that will stay alive and regenerate come the first shower of rain. Only newly sown lawns or those being established from turf should be watered to prevent them dying before your very eyes. So use a sprinkler only on the newest of lawns.

Rainwater always seems to be more to plants' liking than mains water, but the latter is most certainly preferable to no water at all. Hard water may turn the leaves of rhododendrons and other lime haters yellow, so where possible collect rainwater for them.

> **TOP TIP**
>
> Watering takes time, so choose plants that are tolerant of a certain amount of dryness at the roots if you want to minimise the time you spend watering. Plants in containers need regular watering, so the more you have, the more time you'll need to spend watering them – up to twice a day in high summer.

Watering containers

The type of container you choose will have a bearing on the amount of watering it needs. The larger the container, the more slowly it will dry out, so try to avoid having masses of tiny pots on a patio or terrace – they will make you a slave to the hosepipe or watering can. The compost will dry out far too fast and the plants will suffer as a result.

Terracotta and ceramic containers tend to remain cooler than those made of plastic. Ceramic containers dry out more slowly than unglazed terracotta. Peat-free composts need to be kept evenly moist at all times. If they dry out, they shrink from the sides of the pot and re-wetting them can be difficult. Try using a mixture of peat-free soil-based and multi-purpose peat-free compost, which tends to slow down the drying process and reduce shrinkage, as well as adding weight for stability.

Right: Water veg and new plants regularly in hot weather

When planting up containers, don't fill them to the brim. Leave a gap between the surface of the compost and the rim of the pot to allow for watering. Apply water until the pot overflows.

Plant outdoor containers densely. Although this will fill the container with roots, it will slow down evaporation from the surface of the compost.

Watering in the evening is the preferred time of day, so the water will be absorbed under cover of darkness when evaporation rates are at their lowest.

To test the dryness of potting compost, look at it, feel it with your finger or weigh the pot in your hand. If the compost feels like a freshly wrung-out flannel, it is sufficiently moist. Wait until the surface is slightly dry before you soak the compost again.

To look after your containers when you go on holiday, you can invest in a spaghetti system of irrigation pipes for larger containers on a terrace or patio, linked to a timer attached to the tap. Alternatively seek out an obliging neighbour who is happy to check them each day in return for the harvest from your veg patch!

Below left: Water windowboxes daily in summer

Below right: Liquid feed can be diluted in your watering can

FEEDING

All plants need nutrients to stay in the best possible health. Choose from a variety of feeds and natural ways to boost them. Dosage rates and timings vary depending on the plants so read the instructions carefully.

Why feed plants?

Feeding helps to keep plants healthy and encourages flowering and fruiting. Although plants produce their own food through photosynthesis and from the soil, all fruit and vegetables, annual plants and plants in pots will benefit from a regular boost.

Always check the packaging for the correct rate of application.

The basic nutrients plants need

○ Nitrogen (N) for leaf and stem growth
○ Phosphorous (P) for roots
○ Potassium (K) for flowers, fruit and all-round healthy growth

TYPES OF FEED

– Liquid feeds
Mixed with water these are easy to apply and fast-acting as roots can immediately take in the dissolved nutrients in the water. They include high-potassium tomato feeds that are watered in every couple of weeks through summer to promote fruiting.

– Granular and powder feeds
These feed plants slowly and are easy to apply – just mix into compost, sprinkle over the top or push under the surface. They are usually applied when planting or in spring to feed plants through the growing season and include slow-release fertiliser and fish, blood and bone.

– Manure
Well-rotted cattle and horse manures are full of nutrients and can be mixed in with the soil when planting or used as a surface mulch that will eventually break down.

– Compost
Composting garden and kitchen waste, such as dead flowers and leaves and vegetable peelings and eggshells, recycles the nutrients they contain back into the soil for your plants.

PLANT CARE DOS

○ Aim water at the roots rather than soaking the whole plant.

○ Re-use grey water from baths and sinks, but make sure you use only eco-friendly detergents.

○ Collect and store rainwater in open pots or tanks in a place where they can catch it, or divert gutters and downpipes into butts.

○ Feed plants through the growing season.

○ Keep deadheading to keep your flowers in bloom.

○ Collect and store as much rainwater as you can to avoid having to use the mains.

PLANT CARE DON'TS

○ Don't walk on a frozen lawn.

○ Don't leave lawn clippings in heaps on the lawn – this will kill off the grass rather than encouraging it to grow.

○ Don't feed a wilting plant – water first, then feed the next day.

○ Don't prune without checking the particular needs of the plant.

Jargon buster

Deadheading – removing faded flowers to prevent them setting seed – it encourages further flowers and tidies up the plant.

Shoot – growth that emerges from a bud. Usually refers to fresh new growth.

Stem – a plant's main growth above the ground that carries flowers buds, branches and leaves.

Scarifying – removing moss and thatch from your lawn.

Thatch – a dead layer in a lawn, made up of old grass clippings, moss and debris.

Actions:
- Keep on top of lawncare, especially in spring and autumn
- Label new plants or keep a record of what you have planted where, so you can look up how to prune later if you forget the plant's name
- Research your plant's pruning requirements
- Feed plants during summer
- Water containers regularly, daily in summer

CHAPTER EIGHT

Think ahead

Think ahead

Gardeners are innate optimists – always planting for their future pleasure, safe in the knowledge that this year will be better than the last. Planting bulbs in autumn or sowing salads every two weeks to ensure you get a harvest throughout the summer is a present to your future gardening self. In autumn planting bulbs might not seem like a pressing item on your to do list, but come spring you will appreciate all the effort you put in when your containers and borders are full of tulips (see page 80 for how to plant).

As well as planting for the next season, it's worth doing jobs that will help you in the future – this includes making compost to enrich your borders, taking cuttings to make more plants for free and protecting your plants from winter weather.

Core skills:
– Sowing successionally
– Making compost
– Taking softwood cuttings
– Protecting plants from winter weather

5 steps to success

1. **In October and early November,** spend time tending to those plants you know will need your help, whether that involves bringing them under cover, giving them a mulch or wrapping them in fleece. It need not take a long time, especially if the job is spread over a few weekends.

2. **Make your own compost.** Homemade compost boosts fertility. It also enhances the moisture-holding capability of sandy soil by binding particles together and, conversely, improves the drainage of clay soil by forcing its tiny particles apart. It all sounds magical and indeed it is to some extent, although it's magic founded on common sense and practicality.

3. **Think ahead to the next season** when sowing and planting, to help get year-round colour and interest.

4. **Use winter to look through seed and plant catalogues** and work out what you want to sow and plant in the coming seasons.

5. **Keep an eye on the weather forecast** in case of early or late frosts that could damage tender plants or the blossom of fruit trees in the spring.

Right: Placing fleece over a veg bed as protection against cold weather

Ways to plan ahead

Here are a few ways you can plant or sow ahead to make sure there's plenty of colour and interest to look forward through the year. Other tasks such as making compost and protecting plants will pay off in the months to come.

SPRING

- Plant summer-flowering bulbs
- Sow annuals for summer flowers
- Sow veg seed like salad every 2–3 weeks for a continuous supply
- Start a compost bin

SUMMER

- Do the Chelsea chop to delay flowering
- Sow autumn flowering bulbs
- Sow winter salads
- Take cuttings to increase your plant collection for next year

AUTUMN

○ Plant spring-flowering bulbs

○ Put winter protection in place in case of early frosts

○ Reduce the height of shrub and bush roses that have grown very tall by a third to avoid windrock. You can prune properly late winter to spring

WINTER

○ Plant bare-root shrubs and trees

○ Clean the greenhouse ready for spring

○ Clean pots to prevent diseases in the next season

○ Order seeds

Focus on successional sowing

Planning ahead with your crops helps to ensure a continuous supply and avoid gluts. This fantastic technique allows you to spread out harvests. For root vegetables like carrots and beetroot, sow a new row every three weeks, and the same timing applies for peas and dwarf beans.

For salads, sow a new row (or pot) every couple of weeks. This allows a mostly constant supply of the same crop over an extended time period. Another form of succession planting also enables gardeners to get two or three crops from the same area over the growing season; for example, after harvesting new potatoes, you transplant dwarf beans, then harvest those in early September and immediately sow winter radish. Rather than planting the same crop, there is a succession of different crops growing in the same location. Some productive succession plantings to try out are leeks following potatoes, dwarf beans following garlic, and kale following broad beans.

Do the Chelsea chop

The Chelsea chop (so named because its timing coincides with the Chelsea Flower Show) is a method of pruning to bring late summer-flowering perennials under a little more control. By removing the dominant growing tip of the stems, you'll get a bushier, more compact plant that needs less staking later in the year. Carry out the pruning after the risk of frost has passed, when the plant is in active growth but before flower buds start to form. Aim to remove a third or even half of the growth. Doing this will also delay flowering by a month or two, but you will usually get more flowers as a result.

1. Select a suitable late-summer flowering perennial, such as an upright-growing sedum (*Hylotelephium*) or a tall echinacea, helenium, *Phlox paniculata* or penstemon.

2. Make your cuts between a third and half the way down each stem, as evenly as possible all over the plant. As with any pruning, always cut just above a leaf joint.

Below: Doing the Chelsea chop on a sedum (Hylotelephium)

3. Aim to create a well-balanced, rounded clump. Although it will look different from before, you shouldn't be able to see from a mile off that something has been hacked.

Simple propagation

Even keen gardeners who really know their plants can be daunted by propagation – making new plants. Whether this is down to lack of knowledge or confidence, it's a task that sounds more difficult than it is. Taking cuttings is a satisfying job and a surprisingly simple process. And if you do lose a few cuttings, it doesn't really matter – they are only trimmings from your plant. Most of the time, they will root readily and grow into lovely little plants – free plants – that you can give away or use to boost the displays in your garden.

The easiest cuttings for a beginner are softwood cuttings. Softwood cuttings are those taken in spring and early summer from the young, fast-growing tips of plants. Shrubs, perennials and tuberous species, such as dahlias, are all suitable candidates.

The great thing about softwood cuttings is that they're full of vigour and can root faster and more successfully than any other type of cutting. But they are more susceptible to water loss, so conditions have to be good for them to survive. The trick is to take your cuttings early in the morning when the stems are cool and full of water. Trim and pot them up swiftly, or pop them in a plastic bag or some water until you're ready. It's essential to maintain high humidity around the cuttings. Don't overwater, though, as this can cause your cuttings to rot. Start off with something straightforward, like a pelargonium or penstemon.

Left: Potting up a rooted fuchsia cutting to grow it on

HOW TO TAKE SOFTWOOD CUTTINGS

🕐 20 MINUTE TASK
BEST TIME TO DO: MARCH–AUGUST

You will need:
- Cuttings
- Knife
- Small pot
- Peat-free potting compost
- Watering can
- Small plastic bag
- Elastic band

1. Take a cutting from your plant that is around 8cm long – cut just below a leaf node. Remove all but the top four or so leaves with a sharp, sterile knife or blade. If the remaining top leaves are large, halve them to reduce water loss.

2. Fill a small plastic pot with peat-free potting compost to within 1cm of the top. Lightly firm the compost to remove any air gaps. Slide the cuttings down the side of the pot between the plastic and the compost.

3. Firm the cuttings to ensure good contact between soil and root. Label the cuttings, taking note of the plant name and the date you took them. This way you'll know when to start looking out for new roots.

4. Water the cuttings well to ensure that the compost is in good contact with the roots. Place the pot in either an unheated propagator or put an upturned freezer bag over the pot and seal it with an elastic band. Both techniques ensure high humidity for the first few weeks, which will reduce water loss from the cutting and aid rooting.

Dividing plants

Another easy way to make new plants is to split plants that have got too big. This might not be necessary if you're just getting started in gardening, but is a useful technique to remember for a few years down the line. It's a great way to increase your plant stocks and save money. Some perennials will become congested, with all the vibrant flowering growth on the outside of the plant and little interest in the middle. Others can take over the border. Digging them up and dividing them will rejuvenate tired perennials and reduce the size of others.

Divide summer-flowering perennials in autumn or spring, and spring-flowering perennials just after flowering to give them time to establish before the next year. Dig them up with a spade, taking care to keep as much of the roots attached as possible. Then push two garden forks back to back into the centre of the plant and use them as levers to tease the rootball apart – you could also cut through the middle with a knife or spade. When you replant your new bits of plant, make sure you keep them well watered.

EASY PLANTS TO DIVIDE:

- Hardy geraniums
- Hostas
- Asters
- Lily of the valley
- Bergenia

Making compost

It's such a waste not to use your plant waste – far from being useless and unwanted, your garden leftovers can become a positive benefit to your soil. That's what composting is: processing garden waste into something of value, not only to your patch of earth, but also in terms of caring for the environment. It may seem like such a little thing – to rot down your garden's surplus organic matter – but once you've got into the habit of it, you'll wonder why you ever squandered such a valuable resource.

Homemade compost is useful, its production involves little financial outlay, it helps to conserve our valuable peatlands by not depleting them and it will save you the expense of acquiring other forms of soil enrichment. Where once you bought the stuff in plastic sacks, with a little planning and effort you can become self-sufficient. Your soil will benefit, your pocket will benefit and you'll feel supremely virtuous!

Garden soil always contains some organic matter, but because this keeps on rotting down until it disappears completely, it should be replenished on a regular – usually annual – basis. To make your own garden compost, you'll need a compost bin to keep everything in, ideally one metre square and high. Two bins are even better, so you can be filling one while using the rotted contents of the other, once your system is up and running. Make the bins from wooden posts and wire netting, or with slatted wooden sides that are removable, for easy access.

There are two main composting methods – hot and cold. Hot composting involves filling the bin to the brim with a mix of organic matter, then turning it regularly so that rotting is rapid and heat builds up. Plant material that is no longer growing starts to rot. It's up to us to utilise that capability and not to get in the way.

Cold composting takes longer, but doesn't need turning. Just fill the bin gradually when organic waste becomes available. As this decomposes, it heats up, but not as rapidly as with the hot system. It will still rot down well over the course of six months to a year. With the cold system you can fill your compost heap between spring and autumn, then empty it during winter and the following spring.

HOW TO MAKE COMPOST

🕐 5–10 MINUTE TASK

BEST TIME TO DO: YEAR ROUND

What to put in
- Green waste from the veg patch
- Bedding plants, at the end of the season
- Soft green prunings
- Faded flowerheads
- Crushed eggshells
- Torn-up newspaper
- Annual weeds
- Grass clippings (but mix them in!)
- Autumn leaves in small quantities
- Vegetable kitchen waste, such as carrot tops and potato peelings

What to leave out
- Diseased plant material
- Cooked food (including bread and mashed potato)
- Thick-rooted perennial weeds
- Annual weeds that have run to seed
- Thick, woody stems (unless shredded)
- Large amounts of autumn leaves (make leafmould from them separately)

1. **Mix the contents evenly** as you add them, with no big concentration of any one material in any one place – lawn mowings, for example, turn slimy or white and fungus ridden if not mixed with larger-leaved waste. Aim for a 50:50 blend of carbon (generally drier, brown material) and nitrogen (green waste). Chop up or shred woody stems so they decompose faster. You can buy or hire a shredder and if you're a confirmed composter you'll find it wonderfully rewarding.

2. **Keep the contents moist** – in spells of hot, dry weather, give your bin a good watering. In order to continue rotting down, moisture is essential. If the contents dry out, the composting process will slow down or stop altogether.

3. **Firm it down from time to time** – either tamp down the bin's contents with the back of a fork or rake or climb in and tread it down. Air pockets slow the composting process and cause material to dry out in patches, so rotting will be uneven.

4. **Cover the top** with a square of old carpet or sacking to keep the moisture in and help to retain the heat.

Winter protection

During summer, it's easy to forget that many plants in our gardens will suffer from severe cold in the coming months. Most of those that are regarded as 'hardy' will come though unscathed, but others are borderline cases whose survival is dictated by the severity of the winter.

The hazards of winter include low temperatures (with a suddenness that can lead to death), prolonged waterlogging and drying winds. But there are precautions you can take to maximise the survival of all your plants – the secret is to understand their levels of hardiness and to ensure that all reasonable precautions are taken to see them though until spring.

Some will need extra protection by bringing them under cover, providing insulation where they are growing, or moving them to a more sheltered spot in the garden where temperatures are unlikely to plummet to a fatal level.

PLANT HARDINESS GUIDE

Tender
Any plant, like a canna, that is not only killed by frost but sometimes by low temperatures. Such plants need protection in every season except summer, when most can be moved outdoors.

Half-hardy
Any plant, such as cosmos, that is not reliably frost-hardy (it may stand a degree or two of frost but not with any frequency). They need to be raised under glass before being moved outdoors when danger of frost has passed.

Hardy
A plant that is resistant to freezing temperatures. This may mean that its entire above-ground structure survives (as in trees and shrubs), or that in winter it dies back to a perennial rootstock that persists underground, sending up new shoots in spring.

MAKE A PLANT PROTECTION PLAN

Bring indoors

Potted plants that are tender can be brought into a greenhouse that is kept frost free. If you don't have a greenhouse, consider using the bright windowsill of a bedroom for smaller potted treasures. Just don't forget to water them. *Examples:* citrus fruits, pelargoniums

Lift bulbs/tubers

Dig up tender bulbs and tubers, dry them off and store them in trays of dry compost in your shed. Alternatively, cut them down and mulch the ground with a 5cm thick layer of manure, compost or chipped bark, which may offer ample insulation if you do not live in an area that gets heavy frosts. *Examples:* dahlias, gladioli

Insulation

Some plants can be wrapped in fleece for protection. Bubble wrap can be used on clay pots, but avoid swathing plants in this since it doesn't breathe – a build-up of moisture can lead to fungal attack. *Examples:* echiums, tree ferns, plants in terracotta pots

Cloches

Smaller plants, such as winter salads, can be covered with cloches. These will not raise temperatures to a great degree but they will effectively keep out rain and reduce the effects of wind chill. *Examples:* damp sensitive alpines such as raoulia, and grey foliage plants

Move pots

Moving potted outdoor plants closer to the walls of your house will offer them more protection than you would imagine – the brick or stone acts a bit like a storage heater, raising the surrounding temperature ever so slightly at night. *Examples:* potted Japanese maples

Leave unpruned

Think before cutting down all your herbaceous perennials, as some will benefit from the insulation their dry stems and leaves provide. Also, consider wildlife. Birds find seedheads a valuable food resource, and insects hibernate in hollow stems and among dry leaves. *Examples:* eryngiums, grasses, hydrangeas

Top tips for getting ahead in the rest of the garden

– **Make leafmould** Clear leaves from the lawn so they don't simply sit and rot – left on the grass to decay they will kill out great swathes of grass. Use them, instead, to make leafmould that can be returned to the soil. Rot them down in a wire-netting bin constructed in a corner of the garden. It may take a year or so for the leaves to turn into brown and crumbly soil enrichment, but it will be well worthwhile.

– **Protect garden furniture** Such items can be expensive. If it is sturdy and constructed of teak it can be left where it is, but consider oiling it before the worst of the weather sets in to give it greater protection from the weather. Bring under cover more lightweight chairs and tables, giving them a clean before storing them under a dust cover.

– **Wash greenhouse panes** Greenhouses with dirty glass reduce valuable winter light levels dramatically. While the weather is still mild, empty them of plants, scrub down the glass inside and out, and wash staging and gravel.

Give your plants a good picking over to remove faded leaves and flowers, and thus reduce pest and disease attack, then put the plants back inside.

– **Scrub paving slabs** These go green in wet weather. Start off by scrubbing them with a stiff brush and remove stubborn algae with a pressure washer.

– **Clean timber decking** This can be pressure washed to remove slippery algae, and they'll benefit from an application of timber preservative on a dry day. You will increase its life expectancy by treating it every autumn.

– **Add a floating ball to ponds** This will stop them from completely freezing. Make a bigger hole with boiling water to allow fish to breathe in winter.

THINKING AHEAD DOS

○ Try successional sowing with quick-maturing crops like salad, radishes and spring onions.

○ Do get into the habit of composting organic waste and returning it to your soil each spring. It's free and will improve your borders.

○ Take cuttings of plants that are at risk of damage by cold weather – this is good insurance should you lose any plants over winter.

THINKING AHEAD DON'TS

○ Put uncooked meat into a compost bin.

○ Leave tender plants in pots outdoors over winter.

Jargon buster

Propagate – make new plants from seed or cuttings.

Cuttings – a piece (shoot, stem or root) taken from a plant to make a new plant.

Actions:
- Try the Chelsea chop to get bushier plants with more flowers
- Sow crops like salads every two to three weeks for continuous crops
- Take cuttings to boost your plant stocks
- Divide overgrown plants
- Start a compost bin
- Protect tender plants from winter weather
- Look ahead to the next season (eg. plant bulbs in the autumn for spring flowers)

CHAPTER NINE

Gardening with nature

Gardening with nature

For beginners, the benefit of gardening with nature is that over time you will create a balanced garden that attracts predators for garden pests. Gardens are living organisms that can – and should – support many forms of wildlife. Each living thing in your patch is part of a complex food chain that gardeners have a duty to maintain, and that duty comes with many rewards: you will marvel at the blackbird's song, the whirr of a dragonfly across a garden pond and the earthworms that incorporate organic matter into your soil. Greenfly feed ladybirds, slugs feed frogs and thrushes: it is worth learning to tolerate the wildlife that irritates in order to have a vibrant, healthy garden.

Gardening in a wildlife-friendly way means giving up chemicals. Every single creature depends to some extent on another for its survival. Wipe out part of this complex food chain with pesticides and something else is affected. There will always be fluctuations in populations of greenfly, garden birds and amphibians such as frogs and toads, but nature tends to be quite good at maintaining a balance. It takes a while to achieve that balance if you've always sprayed this and that, but you'll find that your outdoor space is soon full of birds, bees, butterflies, insects and microscopic creatures, which all fulfil a vital role in this complex scenario.

As the seasons change, so will the wildlife population in your garden. Some birds – such as swallows – will migrate to warmer climes, while others – such as redwings – will arrive to feed in winter. This rich tapestry of wildlife is ours to enjoy if only we take a little trouble to encourage it.

Core skills:
– Make a container pond
– Plant for pollinators
– Make a bee hotel

5 steps to success

(1) **Grow plenty of single flowers** (those with an open structure), rich in pollen and nectar, to attract insects such as bees that will ensure good crops of peas, beans, apples and pears. Butterflies will be attracted to them, too.

(2) **Feed garden birds** – especially in winter. Not only are they a joy to have around but they also play a vital role in pest control – listen to the tap-tap-tapping of a song thrush breaking a snail shell to eat the tender contents! Put up a nest box. This will encourage bluetits which feed on insect pests.

(3) **A small pond** will bring innumerable forms of life to your garden. Pond skaters will appear from nowhere. How did they know you had just made a pond? Frogs, toads and newts are a delight to watch and will help to control pests. The water will provide sustenance for garden birds and hedgehogs as they come to drink.

(4) **Instead of using insecticides** on vegetables (hardly appetising) use mechanical means of control: fine mesh netting over carrots to deter carrot fly; slightly wider mesh netting over cabbages and other brassicas to prevent large white butterflies laying their eggs and pigeons from tearing at the leaves. Grow raspberries and strawberries in a fruit cage to encourage birds to go elsewhere – all this will provide you with fruit and veg unsullied by noxious sprays.

(5) **Use companion planting to deter pests.** Companion planting is something which has been around for years – the growing of one plant alongside another for mutual benefit. Try planting small-flowered French marigolds (*Tagetes*) in the same soil as your tomatoes. This can help to deter whitefly. Onions planted among carrots will confuse carrot fly due to their strong aroma.

Right: Companion planting helps deter pests from vegetables

Friend or foe?

No garden has the perfect balance between wildlife which is friendly, beautiful and non-destructive, and the more undesirable forms which are a pain in the neck. Try to be realistic about this and not too controlling in the hope of achieving perfection.

Without a few greenfly on your roses, how will bluetits feed their young and how will the ladybirds and lacewings survive? No one loves slugs except toads and thrushes, but mechanical means (copper collars and sharp grit) will reduce their predations, or you can grow less susceptible plants. Worms are vital to garden health – their irritating casts can be swept off the lawn with a birch broom before mowing to stop them becoming mud pats.

It is, in many instances, a matter of adjusting your mindset so that the creatures you see as pests become less important than the many birds, butterflies, bees and mammals that are vital to your garden's existence, and huge contributors to the pleasures of tending it.

HOW CAN WILDLIFE HELP?

Keep an eye – and ear – out for these garden visitors. The more you garden for wildlife, the more you'll see of these creatures.

Robin

The gardener's friend. A voracious eater of insect pests and a constant companion to anyone cultivating soil. Without the robin our gardens would be all the poorer, visually as well as biologically.

Hedgehog

More common in urban areas, hedgehogs feed on worms and invertebrates. Provide shelter for them in the form of hedgehog houses, and never light a bonfire without first checking that they are not sheltering beneath it.

Frog

Useful in controlling slugs and other pests. Frogs will enjoy a garden pond, depositing their spawn in the shallows in late winter and early spring – a great way to get children started in understanding the wonders of nature.

Earthworm

Earthworms are vital for creating healthy soil. They aid drainage and help to incorporate rotting organic matter to enrich the earth, as well as being a food supply for garden birds.

Butterflies

There are so many of these beauties – from small tortoiseshells and red admirals to the earliest brimstone and painted ladies. Single flowers with plenty of pollen and nectar will encourage them and food plants for their caterpillars are vital, too. A patch of nettles in a sunny spot will support several different kinds.

Bumblebee

Without bees we are lost. They are vital pollinators of flowers – ensuring seed is set and that fruit and vegetable crops yield a generous harvest. Relax on removing lawn weeds such as clover and dandelion, which are both rich sources of nectar.

Wasp

Not the enemy that many seem to imagine. Wasps have a healthy appetite and do their bit to keep down greenfly and other insect pests of flowers, fruit and veg.

Spider

As any child knows, spiders eat flies, and flies can be garden pests but are good to feed other wildlife. A spider's web silvered with dew is one of the rewards of getting up early in the morning.

Newt

Garden ponds have become a stronghold for newts – lizard-like amphibians that are one of the treasures of an organic garden, offering children in particular a taste of the age of dinosaurs!

Blackbird

A glorious songster, especially in the evening when it sings from the chimney-tops. Also useful in foraging for grubs in the lawn, provided the grass is short.

10 plants for pollinators

Even a small patch in a tiny garden can make a huge difference to pollinators – the key is to choose the right plants. Go for those with nectar-rich, single flowers rather than blousy double blooms, which are harder for pollinators to get into and may not contain any nectar or pollen. Aim for a broad range of plants that flower early and late in the season, so you provide nectar and pollen for as long as possible – both native and non-native plants can provide food.

1. Wallflower
Flowering almost constantly, *Erysimum* 'Bowles's Mauve' is one of the best pollinator plants you can buy. It provides a long nectar season for moths, butterflies and lots of bee species. Plants spread to over 50cm wide, so you just need one and it will flower from February to the end of summer.

2. Crocus
All spring-flowering crocus provide early nectar for bees emerging from hibernation on warm spring days. Either buy them as potted plants when they're in flower and plant straight away, or wait until September and plant them as bulbs to flower the following year.

3. Hellebore
All hellebores are an important nectar source for bumblebees and other pollinators when they come out of hibernation and are in need of an instant energy boost. Blooming from mid-winter to mid-spring, they are widely available in garden centres.

4. Clematis
Make as much use of your small space as you can by exploiting the vertical areas too. There are lots of pollinator-friendly climbers to choose from, including *Clematis cirrhosa* 'Freckles', which flowers in winter and is a great source of early pollen. You can train it up a metal obelisk if you like, but it'll be fine against a sunny wall too.

5. Marjoram
Its mass of tiny flowers makes this herb a hot favourite with all pollinators, but particularly butterflies and bumblebees in the summer. Put young plants in the back corner of the patch. Pinch out the top of the stem down to the third pair of leaves to encourage the plants to become bushy.

Right: *Crocus tommasinianus*

Below: *Clematis cirrhosa* 'Freckles'

Left: Wild marjoram (*Origanum vulgare*)

Below: *Dahlia* 'Roxy' is the perfect variety for pots at only 45cm high

Above: The double-flowered cosmos 'Fizzy White' flowers for months

Right: Honeysuckle 'Rhubarb and Custard'

6. Honeysuckle

This scrambling climber comes into flower in mid-summer. The blooms are rich in nectar for bumblebees and butterflies and have a strong nocturnal scent to attract night-pollinating moths like the hummingbird hawk moth. Plant at the base of an obelisk or trellis and tie in the stems to guide it.

7. Sedum

A valuable source of late nectar at the end of summer and throughout autumn, this is particularly favoured by male bumblebees and butterflies. Plant small plants of this perennial now and they will burst into bloom in August, then die back in winter and regrow next year.

8. Dahlia

These prolific flowerers bloom until the first frosts. Look for varieties with simple open flowers, such as those with 'Bishop' in the name, that allow bees, hoverflies and butterflies to access the nectar easily. Buy potted plants and keep undercover somewhere frost-free until late May–June.

9. Cosmos

Manna for insects, these flower from June until the first frosts. Either sow directly into your patch or sow in small pots to give them a head start against slugs or buy young plants and plant out after the last frosts.

10. Gaura

The small flowers, on tall, thin stems, are visited by pollinators with long tongues, such as butterflies and bumblebees, but it is also a night bloomer that is a valuable nectar source for moths. Buy as young plants in spring and they will flower throughout the summer.

Right: *Sedum* 'Autumn Joy' (Hylotelephium)

HOW TO MAKE A SOLITARY BEE HOTEL

🔵 60 MINUTE TASK
BEST TIME TO DO: LATE
MARCH–EARLY APRIL

You will need:
– Block of untreated wood
– Drill and drill bits (1mm to 10mm in diameter)
– A screw to fix the hotel to a fence post
– Sandpaper

Solitary bees are beneficial pollinators who love to nest in trees and shrubs where there is dead wood. You can help them find a safe nesting spot by making this simple bee hotel.

1. Place the wood on a firm surface and use a variety of drill bits to create different sized holes.

2. Roll sandpaper into a tube and use to sand each hole, making sure there are no snags on the inside.

3. Thoroughly sand the block's surface, too, so insects won't catch on any splinters.

4. Simply screw to a secure post and wait for visitors to arrive.

3 ways to help wildlife

LET HEDGEHOGS IN AND OUT

Man-made boundaries are meaningless to wild creatures, which often need to roam far and wide to seek out food and mates. Hedgehogs, for example, will cover about a mile every night. To provide passages between boundaries, you could remove a brick from the base of a wall, dig a small channel below a hedge or cut a rectangular, or circular, hole measuring 13cm x 13cm in the base of a fence. This will be big enough for hedgehogs to move around freely but too small for most pets to get through.

FEED THE BIRDS

Gardens naturally supply seeds, berries and insects for birds and wildlife, but providing extra food will help supplement their diets through the lean times in winter and in hot, dry summers. Fill feeders with a range of sunflower hearts, niger seeds, suet and peanuts, as different food suits different birds, and hang them all year round in trees and bushes well away from potential predators.

MAKE A BUG HOTEL

A bug hotel filled with natural materials from the garden can become an attractive feature and provide valuable shelter for ladybirds, solitary bees, beetles; even toads and hedgehogs. The residents you attract will depend on whether it is placed in the sun or shade. Pile up tiles, pine cones, bark, dead leaves and stones, and layer stacks of bamboo canes and hollow plant stems horizontally to stop water dripping inside. The cracks and crevices they create will become welcome nooks where wildlife can rest and breed.

HOW TO MAKE A CONTAINER POND

HALF DAY TASK
BEST TIME TO DO: SPRING

You will need:

- Container, such as a Belfast sink
- Old piece of pond liner or sturdy plastic (old compost bag is fine)
- Bathroom sealant
- Bricks, or similar, for supporting plants and making the frog ladder
- Plants (such as brooklime, water forget-me-not, spiked water milfoil, hornwort)
- Water (rainwater is preferable but tap water is fine)

You don't need a large garden to make a wildlife pond. A simple container pond – using an old Belfast sink or similar vessel – makes the perfect habitat for a wide range of species. While large ponds attract the most wildlife, smaller ponds still attract frogs, newts, dragonflies, damselflies and other invertebrates.

To make your container pond as wildlife-friendly as possible, add a couple of native marginals, such as brooklime and water-forget-me-not, as well as oxygenating plants, like hornwort and spiked water milfoil. Aim for around two-thirds of the pond's surface to be covered with plants. Place bricks or other materials at the pond's edge to make a 'frog ladder' so that amphibians can climb in.

Place the pond in partial shade – ideally so it gets sun in spring but shade in summer – and the water will warm up in colder months, but not dry out in the heat. You could also sink the pond into the ground, to maintain an even temperature.

1. Cut the pond liner to size so it fits snugly in the bottom of the container. Use sealant around the edges to make it watertight. Leave to dry.

2. Partially fill the pond with water to check it's watertight. Drain, dry and add more sealant if necessary. It's important to get this one right.

3. Add bricks on either side of the pond to support your marginal pond plants. This creates different water depths in the pond, making it a better wildlife habitat.

4. Stand marginal plants on the bricks. The top of each pot should sit just below the rim of the pond, so it doesn't protrude when the pond is filled with water.

5. Fill your pond with water, ensuring the marginal plants sit well when the container is full. Add oxygenating plants that float just beneath the surface.

6. Add bricks or other materials to the outside of the container to make a frog ladder. Don't worry if there's still a gap at the top of the container – frogs can climb.

WILDLIFE GARDENING DOS

○ Leave a clump of nettles to grow – these are a vital food source for various caterpillars, including those of the small tortoiseshell and red admiral butterflies.

○ Top up bird baths and ponds in hot weather.

○ Choose a location for ponds that is in partial shade to prevent excess algae growth.

○ Aim for a broad mix of leafy marginals, grassy marginals, floating plants, oxygenators and water lilies in ponds to support the widest diversity of wildlife.

○ If you have a pond in your garden, ensure hedgehogs and other wildlife have safe, easy access by creating a gradual slope at one end.

○ Grow a mix of plants, including shrubs, small trees and climbers travelling up obelisks to provide a higher canopy, with perennials and groundcover plants for smaller insects, ground-feeding birds and mammals.

WILDLIFE GARDENING DON'TS

○ Don't be in too much of a hurry to tidy up in the autumn – many caterpillars and pupae hibernate on the ground and among dead foliage.

○ Don't import water from another pond or water source. It may help increase diversity but can also introduce disease.

○ Don't put in a fountain if you want water lilies – they object to growing in turbulent water.

○ Do not add fish to a wildlife pond, which will eat frog and toad spawn, but choose a range of deep-water, floating, marginal and oxygenating plants to give cover and shelter.

○ Don't cut mature ivy back too early as the flowers provide a late source of nectar and pollen for insects and the foliage will shelter hibernating wildlife.

Actions:
– Put up a bird feeder to help birds through winter and encourage a wider variety into your garden
– Grow plants that attract pollinators
– Add a wildlife friendly feature to your garden such as a nesting box, bee hotel or pond

CHAPTER TEN

Tackle problems early

Tackle problems early

Left: *Sedum* 'Purple Emperor' and *Echinacea* 'Summer Cocktail'

Beginners are often put off by garden problems such as pests, diseases and weeds. At first glance these can seem like insurmountable obstacles, but the more you know about the problem, the easier it is to deal with. Keeping your plants healthy is the first step, as it will help increase resilience to pests and disease.

Get to know your plants and you'll soon spot if something is wrong – the earlier you spot signs of pests, diseases or weeds, the more likely it is that you'll be able to do something about it. Regular, light weeding is a great way to keep on top of weeds as well as detect early signs of pests, diseases and other problems. You'll notice straight away if a plant is being attacked by pests, ailing from a disease or simply needs water.

In worst case scenarios, you may need to ditch a plant, if the disease is not treatable, but more often than not, there is a solution. Attracting wildlife to the garden will help keep pests to a manageable level, and weeding regularly throughout the season can help tackle even the worst offenders.

Core skills:
– Identifying weeds, pests and diseases
– Learning how to tackle problems

5 steps to success

1. **Mulch beds and borders** each spring to limit annual weeds. In the veg patch, take a tip from commercial organic growers and lay paper or black polythene between rows of crops to smother out weeds.

2. **Grow cultivated plants** close together in well-enriched soil, so they quickly form an impenetrable blanket over the ground, allowing little room for opportunist weeds. Bare earth is an open invitation to outsiders.

3. **Grow your plants well.** Those that are growing in well-nourished soil and are not allowed to go short of food and water are far more likely to shrug off attacks than those that are weak and feeble, struggling in dry earth that is poorly fed and short on supplies of moisture.

4. **Buy new plants from a reputable source** and check that they are pest-free before you take them home.

5. **Sometimes the apparent onset of disease is nothing of the sort.** It's what scientists call a 'physiological disorder' – ill health brought about by a lack of air, too much or too little water at the roots, a mineral deficiency or other unsuitable growing conditions. In most cases, the trick here is to identify and correct the problem.

Right: Plants growing close together leave less room for weeds to take hold

Weeds

There are no two ways about it – gardeners are obsessed with weeds. It's easy to see why: they compete with the plants we love, they appear in every available nook and cranny, and they interfere with the aesthetic appreciation of our well-cultivated plot.

But what exactly is a weed? The precise definition is that a weed is a 'plant growing where it is not wanted', but to most of us a weed is the name we give to any British wildflower (mainly the ugly ones!) that invades our beds and borders. There are annual kinds that seed themselves freely and there are perennials with tenacious roots that are the very devil to eradicate.

Of course, these days native wildflowers must be encouraged in all our gardens to benefit insect life, so cultivating a little tolerance is good for everyone. But some weeds can become a real nuisance.

The challenge for the organic gardener is to control weeds without resorting to chemicals, which, as far as the amateur is concerned, are likely to be phased out soon anyway. Safer by far is to look for alternative means of keeping on top of these plant invaders, other than spraying willy-nilly with noxious fluids that can have a damaging effect on our environment and upset the balance of nature.

Left: Regularly hoeing annual weeds helps keep on top of them

Different types of weed are a problem in different areas of the garden. On the veg plot it's usually annual weeds that are a nuisance – self-seeding and growing rapidly. In beds and borders, where the soil is disturbed less frequently, perennial weeds have the chance to get their roots firmly established.

So, how do you prevent weeding becoming an arduous chore? The big mistake is to keep putting it off. The longer you delay, the worse it gets. Conversely, early weeding is quick and easy – and rewarding. The garden always looks better when treasured plants are not being overrun, or rows of vegetables smothered.

The trouble with weeds is that they are so successful. They outgrow everything, spreading by means of wandering roots (nettles), runners (creeping buttercups) or rhizomes (couch grass). Or they overwhelm by prolific self-seeding (dandelion clocks and thistle seed heads). Most weeds are rampant British wildflowers, which naturally grow faster than more delicate, highly cultivated, foreign plants. Wildflower seeds germinate at lower soil temperatures, which is why weeds are always the first seedlings to appear in spring.

What to do about weeds? The toughest weeds can still be controlled by hand, without making a lot of extra work for yourself, if you go about it the right way. There's nothing you can't get rid of, over time, just by regular hoeing (and that applies even to ground elder and bindweed).

KNOW YOUR WEEDS

Annuals
Annual weeds complete their growing cycle in one season or quicker, so the key is to stop them before they set seed. The most common annual weeds are chickweed, groundsel and hairy bittercress.

They are the easiest to remove, as their roots are found around the surface of the soil. This can be done by hand or with a fork, or by hoeing beds on a regular basis. This frees the roots and it's then easy to clear up by hand. Don't hoe too deeply though as it may bring up ungerminated seeds to the surface. Cover with mulch to suppress their growth.

Perennials
These include couch grass, dandelions and bindweed. They die back in winter and reappear in spring. Their roots go deep into the earth, making them hard to remove – if any pieces of root get left in the soil, they will re-grow into a new plant. Dig them out carefully, concentrating on small areas at a time, and remove every piece of root. Weakening the weed is another method.

Pernicious
These include Japanese knotweed, horsetail and ground elder. They're fast growing, thug-like, damage other plants and take over a garden. If you find Japanese knotweed, there is legislation that covers its control and disposal, so seek professional advice.

FIVE INVASIVE WEEDS

Regular removal helps you keep on top of most weeds, but take care when disposing of them. If you compost your weeds make sure you are using a hot composting method which reaches sufficient temperature to kill seeds and roots.

From left to right:
Bindweed; ground elder
roots; nettles; groundsel

1. Bindweed

A twining weed with thick roots and white trumpet flowers. It scrambles through border plants and shrubs. It will grow back from a tiny piece of root, so you need to remove as much as you can from your border.

What to do: Pull out stems and fork out as much root as possible every time you see it.

2. Horsetail

It looks like little Christmas trees, but has very deep roots and can take over borders.

What to do: It responds to regular pulling and even hoeing, but you have to keep at it for a long time.

3. Ground elder
Green elder-like leaves and white flowerheads. It forms a thick mat of roots and can force out other plants.

What to do: Keep pulling out the thick white roots.

4. Stinging nettle
Tall plants with jagged-edged leaves that have stinging hairs. A good butterfly egg-laying site, but it's best confined to a single sunny corner of the garden.

What to do: Fork out its roots and wear thick gloves.

5. Groundsel
A little green weed with clusters of small yellow flowerheads. It seeds itself about rapidly.

What to do: Hand pull it or hoe out seedlings.

Tackling garden pests

Left: The caterpillar-like larvae of sawfly, feeding on a gooseberry bush

Garden pests are never going to go away. All pest control is a short-term solution so it makes sense for any gardener to find the most environmentally friendly way of controlling pests – a way that respects nature, even if we are trying to bend her to our will. Our gardens are, or should be, a microcosm of the natural world and most of us cherish them for that reason, so it makes sense to interfere with the complex cycle of interdependency as little as possible.

You are never going to banish pests completely, and in a garden run on organic lines they are, like it or not, part of the food chain. Even wasps – which everybody seems to detest, mainly on account of their sting – contribute to pest control as they feed on small insects such as aphids, as well as sugars in the form of nectar and honeydew. Learning to develop a more relaxed approach will not only help lower your blood pressure but, once the food chain has settled into a natural cycle, you will notice fewer epidemics since the natural predators of certain plant-eating or sap-sucking insects will have been allowed to build up in numbers, rather than being discouraged by the use of non-selective insecticides and chemicals.

Even products that only target greenfly and blackfly are by their very nature removing a part of the food chain that supports valuable predators, so even they interfere with the natural order of things. What's important is that you have a garden where occasional rises in the population of certain pests will almost always be temporary, thanks to the intervention of other forms of life that feed on the things we consider 'the baddies' – the plant pests.

WHAT ARE PLANT PESTS?

The creatures we really hate are those that feed on plants in one of several ways. Aphids (greenfly and blackfly) suck sap and by so doing can also transmit viruses that cause a lack of vigour and distortion of leaves and stems. Along with whitefly they also secrete honeydew, which makes leaves sticky and leads to the growth of sooty mould. This covers the leaves with a black felt that not only looks unsightly but also reduces plant vigour, since it cuts out the amount of light reaching the foliage and impedes photosynthesis, a process by which the plant manufactures food.

Then there are the chompers – the caterpillars, slugs and snails – which actually take lumps out of leaves. Caterpillars have sharp mouthparts, whereas slugs and snails have rasping mouthparts that tear out holes rather than cutting them. Neatest of all are leaf-cutter bees, which take pieces of leaf to make nests. You can't do much about them so you might as well come to terms with the fact and admire their industry. They seldom take enough to weaken a rose bush anyway.

SLUGS AND SNAILS

The problem
Plants with succulent leaves (such as hostas), seedlings and young plants with soft and sappy foliage are eaten away, and often only the midrib of the leaf is left intact – hostas can be turned to lace.

The culprits
A wide range of slugs, from the larger brown field slugs that feed above ground to small black keeled slugs that attack potatoes and other roots. On chalky ground, snails are the more common culprits and can demolish plants overnight. Of summer bedding, they are particularly fond of tobacco plants.

The solutions
The most obvious (and most tedious) is hand picking those pests that attack above ground. Slugs and snails hate bright sunshine and hot, dry weather, so the best time to find them is at night with a torch. If you only have a few plants – in pots, perhaps – this is an effective means of control. Take the pests somewhere else if you prefer not to kill them, but remember they have a homing instinct, so take them for a car ride.

Copper collars placed around hostas as their buds push through the surface of the soil in spring are effective, as is copper tape around the rim of pots.

Below left: Snails will feed on seedlings and young plants with soft foliage

Below right: Remove aphids by hand when they colonise veg like broad beans, or wash them off with a hose

Half grapefruits, crushed grit and eggshells spread around plants are rarely a deterrent. Beer traps (empty yoghurt pots sunk into the ground and filled with beer) will catch some slugs and snails, but not all. Biological control in the form of slug-attacking nematodes can be watered on to kill subterranean slugs, but the earth needs to have reached a suitable temperature in spring. Encouraging wildlife makes a difference – remember that frogs and toads will help with slug control (small ones), as will hedgehogs, and song thrushes feed on snails. In severe cases, look to plants that are resistant to attack, such as those with hairy leaves or tough, leathery foliage.

SAP-SUCKING INSECTS

The problem
Plants are weakened, foliage is distorted and bleached, and covered in a sticky honeydew on which thick, black sooty mould thrives. Virus diseases are spread by the mouthparts of pests, which often cluster around the growing point of the plants.

The culprits
Aphids (greenfly and blackfly), whitefly (those small white creatures that look like miniature Concorde aircraft on the undersides of the leaves) and red spider mites (pinprick-sized mites of yellow, green or red) are all to blame, as are mealy bugs, which surround themselves with white wool on greenhouse plants, and scale insects, the pests that look like miniature limpets or legless tortoises.

The solutions
Red spider mites can be discouraged by keeping a moist atmosphere in the greenhouse (they prefer warm, dry conditions) and all greenhouse pests can be kept in check by buying predatory insects, which vary depending on the pest (a chalcid wasp for whitefly, a predatory mite for red spider). Use sticky plastic traps to catch whitefly. Dab scale insects and mealy bugs with a tiny paintbrush dipped in methylated spirits or whisky. For greenfly and blackfly, use your fingers to rub them off or spray them with very mild soapy water, or – on sturdy plants such as roses – squirt them with a powerful jet from a hose. Birds, wasps and ladybirds will do their bit, too.

ROOT-EATING LARVAE

The problem
Plants that looked healthy suddenly wilt and collapse or gradually dwindle in terms of vigour. On inspection, the roots will have been eaten away.

The culprits
Carrot fly will bore into carrot roots (it doesn't always cause the plants to die, but makes the maggoty roots less appetising) and cabbage root fly will eat away the roots of cabbages, which leads to collapse and death. Pot plants such as cyclamen and some plants in the garden are martyrs to vine weevil larvae, which eat the roots and lead to plants collapsing and dying.

The solutions

Position small felt collars around young brassicas when planting to prevent root flies from laying eggs on the soil close to the stems. Sow carrots thinly to avoid needing to thin the seedlings, which releases an aroma that attracts the flies. Sow spring onions alongside them since carrot flies are deterred by the aroma of alliums. Cover carrot rows with crop protection netting. For vine weevil, check plants' roots at potting time and remove the curly maggots by hand. Water plants with biological control nematodes to keep them healthy. Pick off adult weevils, which feed on leaf edges at night.

Above left: Look out for vine weevil larvae in the compost of container-grown plants

Above right: Inspect the underside of leaves for the eggs of cabbage white butterflies

LEAF-EATING LARVAE

The problem

Leaves are eaten and shredded, or have rolled downwards and inwards.

The culprits

All manner of larvae of butterflies, flies and moths, from large and small white butterfly caterpillars on brassicas and nasturtiums, to tortrix moths and sawfly larvae on roses or fruit trees.

The solutions

Hand picking is the obvious one, but also encourage birds and other natural predators to help by putting up feeders and nest boxes. Crop protection netting will protect brassicas by preventing cabbage white butterflies from laying their eggs on the leaves. Moths that damage apples and pears can be caught in sticky pheromone traps hung in the trees. And remember that wasps eat caterpillars!

BUGS AND BEETLES

The problem
Leaves and flowers are eaten by insects with large mouthparts that chew rather than suck sap.

The culprits
Lily beetles (red adults and grubs covered in black frass) attack leaves and flowers of lilies, earwigs (with pincer-like tails) eat dahlia flowers, and assorted other beetles devour a range of plants, including rosemary, mint and viburnum.

The solutions
Often very difficult, since these pests are tough-coated blighters and quick movers. Trap earwigs in flower pots that have been inverted on canes among dahlias and stuffed with straw. Lily beetles can be nipped between finger and thumb (if you are quick enough) and their larvae squirted off with a powerful jet from a hose. Other beetles are more difficult to control, but growing plants that are well fed and not allowed to go short of light and water can make all the difference to their ability to shrug off attacks. Vigilance is helpful in spotting attacks before they get out of hand.

Right: Lily beetles make round holes in the leaves of lilies and fritillaries

Tackling plant diseases

WHAT ARE DISEASES?

Diseases that affect plants, like those that affect humans, fall into three main categories: fungi, bacteria and viruses. In many instances, all three tend to attack plants that are already weak and susceptible to infection. Ensuring plants have ample supplies of light, food and water goes a long way towards keeping them healthy, as does growing them in conditions to which they are suited, be that sun, shade, well-drained soil or moisture-retentive earth. 'Right plant, right place' was never more applicable than in the world of disease-free plants.

Fungi in particular are opportunists that can seek out a weak and struggling plant, especially where conditions offer them the dampness many of them need to thrive. Plants growing in an airless greenhouse, for instance, are more susceptible to botrytis – grey mould – than those in a better-ventilated atmosphere.

Bacteria are especially likely to enter plants through damaged tissue. They can cause the formation of galls (outgrowths due to a proliferation of plant tissue), leaf spots and cankers.

Viruses – also known as plant pathogens – are micro-agents that cause the distortion of leaves and stems, leaf spotting, streaking and discoloration of leaves and flowers. They are incurable and plants that show signs of a virus are often best dug up and burned. This may seem an extreme mode of treatment, but as we know from our own experiences over the last few years, viruses are insidious and can spread readily.

Add to these all the other assorted diseases caused by fungal/algal-like organisms such as *Phytophthora ramorum* – sudden oak death – and you could begin to think that death was lying in wait around every corner of the garden. In a way, this is true, but there is much we can do to ward it off.

HOW TO WORK OUT WHAT'S WRONG

Doing a Sherlock Holmes-style analysis of your plant's problem will often reveal that the conditions in which the plant is growing are responsible for its inability to thrive, far more often than being attributable to any disease. Overwatering, for example, is hard to spot. When plant roots die due to drowning in too much water with no air supply, the plant can wilt, never to recover. This is completely different from a plant that wilts due to dryness at the roots, when a really good soak will cause it to spring back to health within an hour or two. The key is to identify the problem swiftly and go straight into action.

1. Take a close look at any plant that's suffering, along with its growing conditions. Consider the state of the soil (too wet or too dry?)

Right: Honey fungus growing at the bottom of a tree

2. Look at the amount of light it receives (too shady or scorched by sunshine?)

3. Has any there been any likely pollution of the soil (did you spill petrol from the mower?)

4. Has the plant been exposed to strong and drying winds that can 'burn' the foliage? Very low temperatures will persist in a frost-pocket far longer than in areas where the air is free flowing, and tender foliage may suffer as a result.

TACKLING COMMON DISEASES

If it's not one of the problems listed above, look up the type of disease to find out how to tackle it. Here are a few of the common diseases to look out for:

Black spot on roses

This is a fungal disease that is more prevalent when plants are under stress – almost always caused by dryness at the roots.

What to do: enriching the soil with organic matter where roses are to be planted will help to hold on to moisture and ensure steady growth. That explains why roses are renowned for performing better in heavy clay than in light sandy soil. Regular watering in dry weather, along with a moisture-retaining mulch on the soil surface, will help to ward off this disease. Best

Below left: Black spot on rose leaves

Below right: Powdery mildew on sweet peas

of all, choose roses with thick, leathery leaves, which are more resistant to attack in the first place. Gather up and burn any black spot infected leaves at the end of the season to prevent the spores they contain from re-infecting the plant the following year.

Powdery mildew

This often strikes in dry weather. White, powdery material appears on leaf surfaces and flowers. Affected leaves can die. It affects plants including roses, acanthus and phlox, and edibles such as apple and courgettes.

What to do: mulch plants and water regularly but avoid the leaves, directing water at the roots. Remove affected leaves.

Coral spot

This potentially deadly fungus should be treated quickly. Look for orange-coloured pustules on dead woody branches. You'll find it on magnolia and maples, as well as fruit trees and bushes.

What to do: remove and destroy infected wood immediately. Do not shred or add to the compost heap. When pruning, always cut back to healthy wood. Do not leave snags that could become infected. Avoid pruning in damp weather.

Rust

A distinctive fungal infection, which damages leaves, weakening plants. Look out for orange or brown spots on the lower leaf surface. Dying leaves will fall off. This affects many plants, but particularly hollyhocks and roses. Edible plants, such as beans, leeks, apples, pears and raspberries are also at risk.

What to do: remove and destroy infected leaves or grow rust-resistant varieties.

Canker

Various fungal and bacterial diseases cause damage to woody stems. Look for rough raised areas on them. These become swollen and bark splits. Bacterial canker causes sunken patches on stems, which ooze sticky amber-coloured resin. It affects trees and shrubs, including cherries, plums and apples.

What to do: cut out infected branches, then seal cuts with wound paint and sterilise cutting tools.

Potato blight

Sultry conditions in mid-summer, when humidity and temperatures are high for more than 48 hours, can result in something called a Beaumont Period. Under these conditions, potatoes and tomatoes growing outdoors are much more likely to become infected with the fungus we call potato blight, the foliage – and the fruits in the case of tomatoes – becoming blackened.

What to do: there is nothing we can do about this except hope for dry, not humid summers. Dig up and destroy affected plants, although potato tubers may be fine if harvested quickly.

Phytophthora root rot

Yellowing and eventually browning of leaves, wilting, basal decay, rotting roots and dieback are the symptoms of this fungus disease, which affects a wide range of herbaceous plants, conifers and shrubs. It almost always requires waterlogged conditions.

What to do: to minimise the likelihood of this disease, improve the drainage of damp soil by digging in sharp sand and, if necessary, installing a drainage system. Affected plants should be destroyed and the soil replaced before replanting.

Grey mould

Botrytis attacks weak and damaged plant tissue, especially in poorly ventilated greenhouses. The base of cuttings are particularly prone to infection.

What to do: using well-drained sandy potting compost, adequate ventilation and the removal of any fading foliage will do much to reduce its presence.

Honey fungus

This is especially prevalent in old gardens where the soil has been host to plants for years. It mainly affects trees and shrubs, and gets its name from the clusters of honey-coloured toadstools that may sprout at the base of affected plants in autumn. It can cause lack of vigour and eventual death of the plant , and you may also see a white mould between the bark and the

From left to right: Rust on snapdragons; potato blight; honey fungus; brown rot on an apple

wood, which indicates the presence of mycelia. Black rhizomorphs (often known as bootlaces) allow the fungus to travel through the soil.

What to do: dig up and burn affected plants. Then fork through the soil, removing any bootlaces you find, and add organic enrichment to help subsequent plantings flourish.

Brown rot of fruit

Apples and pears – especially those in storage – are susceptible to this fungal disease, which causes them to turn brown and rotten. Tell-tale concentric circles of creamy-white pustules on the surface of the skin are a giveaway. Fruit may shrivel and stay attached to the tree all winter. Damaged fruits are most prone to infection.

What to do: infection may be wind-blown or carried by insects, so remove all infected fruits from the tree and the ground. Bin rotting fruits. To discourage brown rot in future, improve airflow by pruning out damaged, diseased or dead wood. If the crown is congested, thin out a few overcrowded branches to open up the centre of the tree.

Store only fruits with no signs of bruising or broken skin. Space the fruits out so they aren't touching each other – the fungus can spread from one fruit to another by contact. Check stored fruits regularly, discarding any that show symptoms.

Focus on viruses

Left: Plant viruses can cause leaf disfiguration as well as variegation like streaking and yellowing

These are the most insidious of plant diseases, in that there is no cure and plants will never recover. These microscopic pathogens cause disfigurement of leaves, streaking, variegation (many variegated plants owe their leaf coloration to viruses with which they can co-exist) and a reduction in vigour.

Potato leaf curl and tobacco mosaic virus are two of the most common viruses. The latter affects tomatoes, cucumbers and peppers, as well as the plant after which it is named. Poor vigour and a yellowing of leaves between the veins are likely signs. The only course of action is to destroy affected plants.

Many viruses are spread by sap-sucking insects such as aphids, so controlling these can prevent outbreaks. Crop rotation in the garden and veg patch and good hygiene will reduce the incidence of viruses, as will buying certified virus-free plants, bulbs and tubers, especially with seed potatoes, strawberries and raspberries.

PROBLEM SOLVING DOS

○ Tackle problems early, before pests or weeds become too entrenched.

○ Try picking off pests such as snails and aphids to keep down populations.

○ Encourage wildlife to the garden to prey on garden pests.

○ Grow blight and black spot resistant varieties.

○ Weed regularly so that weeds don't steal nutrients and water from your plants.

PROBLEM SOLVING DON'TS

○ Despair if you don't see pest populations decrease the first year – as your garden finds a balance, birds and other wildlife will arrive to eat caterpillars and aphids.

○ Use chemicals.

Jargon buster

Left: Pick off snails to keep populations down.

Below right: Mulch borders and around veg to suppress weeds

Biological control – the use of natural enemies to control pests, using organisms that will feed on or actively discourage the multiplication of another organism. Such predators are available for many pests, from whitefly and red spider mite to slugs and vine weevils.

Actions:
- Mulch borders in spring to keep down weeds
- Keep an eye on plants – when you're walking around the garden watering look out for pest and disease problems.
- Tackle weeds early
- Keep on top of pest populations by picking them off by hand

Project List

PROJECT	BEST TIME TO DO	PAGE NO.
How to test your soil	Year round	25
How to make a garden plan	Year round	64
How to plant bulbs in a pot	October–November	80
How to support new plants	November–May	114
How to sow indoors	January–April	118
How to sow outdoors	April–June	119
How to plant a summer container	June	135
How to plant up a hanging basket	April–June	138
How to chit potatoes	February	158
How to plant fruit trees in a pot	November–March	164
How to prune a shrub rose	February–March	196
How to take softwood cuttings	March–August	215
How to make compost	Year round	220
How to make a solitary bee hotel	Late March–Early April	244
How to make a container pond	Spring	248

Index

Picture credits

BBC Books an imprint of Ebury Publishing
20 Vauxhall Bridge Road
London SW1V 2SA

BBC Books is part of the Penguin Random House group of companies whose addresses can
be found at global.penguinrandomhouse.com

First published by BBC Books in 2024

www.penguin.co.uk

A CIP catalogue record for this book is available from the British Library

ISBN 9781785948978

Commissioning Editor: Phoebe Lindsley
Editorial Assistant: Céline Nyssens
Design: Louise Evans
Production: Antony Heller

BBC Gardeners' World Magazine: Kevin Smith, Tamsin Hope Thomson, Sarah Edwards
Compiled by *BBC Gardeners' World Magazine*

Printed and bound in China by C&C Offset Printing Co., Ltd.

The authorised representative in the EEA is Penguin Random House Ireland, Morrison
Chambers, 32 Nassau Street, Dublin D02 YH68.

Penguin Random House is committed to a sustainable future for our business, our readers
and our planet. This book is made from Forest Stewardship Council® certified paper.